# VOICES IN HARMONY

# VOICES IN HARMONY

## YOUTH CHOIR LEADERSHIP, EDUCATION, AND ARTISTRY

### By Robyn Lana

Foreword by Rollo Dilworth

© 2017 Alfred Music
Printed in the U.S.A.
All Rights Reserved.

ISBN-10: 1-4706-3229-2
ISBN-13: 978-1-4706-3229-8

# TABLE OF CONTENTS

# PREPARING THE PERFORMANCE

# GENDER-SPECIFIC TEACHING

# BEHIND THE SCENES

# APPENDICES

# FOREWORD

ROLLO A. DILWORTH, D. MUS.
PROFESSOR OF CHORAL MUSIC EDUCATION
CHAIR, DEPARTMENT OF MUSIC EDUCATION AND THERAPY
CENTER FOR THE PERFORMING AND CINEMATIC ARTS
BOYER COLLEGE OF MUSIC AND DANCE
TEMPLE UNIVERSITY, PHILADELPHIA, PENNSYLVANIA

In *Voices in Harmony*, Robyn Lana has assembled a prestigious group of choral music educators to develop an innovative resource for those who serve children's and youth choral organizations. Through imaginative curriculum design, creative instructional delivery, a commitment to commissioning new repertoire, and purposeful community engagement, Lana has been a leading advocate for providing quality choral music education experiences to children and youth in the greater Cincinnati area for more than 25 years. And as conductor, teacher, and managing artistic director of one of the top children's and youth choir programs in the nation, Lana is keenly aware of the essential elements necessary for achieving artistic success with young singers.

The book begins with what Lana believes to be the foundational and key ingredient for the success of any choral program: providing a safe, nurturing, and inclusive environment for singers to learn and grow. Lana and the contributing authors—who are all experts in their respective areas—give the reader a rich perspective on a variety of topics, including rehearsal methods, musicianship training, performance preparation, gender-specific teaching, recruitment, preparing major works, and professional collaborations.

*Voices in Harmony* is a uniquely designed guide that offers best practices for building a successful children's or youth choir program. It provides the perfect pathway for educating young choristers in the twenty-first century. I am confident you will find it to be informative, engaging, and inspiring!

# INTRODUCTION

ROBYN LANA

For over 30 years, I have had the privilege of learning from a variety of choral educators and respected colleagues. When I began my volunteer work in the choral field, I was honored to serve colleagues in the children's and youth choir profession: first in Ohio, then regionally, and ultimately nationally when I served as the Children's and Community Youth Choir Repertoire and Standards Chair (now Repertoire and Resources) for the American Choral Directors Association (ACDA). Through serving, I was blessed to meet outstanding educators and conductors internationally. Each one came with training and experiences that I found invaluable. I knew, from the start, that my role at the national level was to bring choral leaders from many philosophies together to learn from each other. It was important to me to include those trained in as many philosophies as possible.

After six years serving ACDA at the national level, it was my hope to compile a resource that would highlight many of those colleagues and philosophies—friends who gave of themselves during my time in service and who celebrated each other and what we each brought to the art form.

This book is just that. I thank each one of these fine artists from the bottom of my heart. This book is not only a gift of their time and talents, but a means of supporting the choral field, with proceeds supporting Chorus America, another organization which I proudly serve, as it works so hard to support community programs in a unique way. Selflessly, the authors in this resource continue to give back not only to their choristers but to the choral community. I know you will find their effort and expertise valuable to your work with children's and youth choirs whether community, school, or church programs.

# THE ENVIRONMENT

## CHAPTER 1

# BUILDING COMMUNITY, A SAFE ENVIRONMENT

BY ROBYN LANA

Every pack has a leader. That leader must be strong, focused, and nurturing, while setting clear expectations, since members of the pack will follow their leader and rely on them for teaching, finding nourishment, and safety. A safe environment is paramount. In a choir, the conductor is the leader and the singers are the pack. Because of this pack mentality, conductors often witness a fear in new singers entering an ensemble. It can be even more apparent when many members of the group have returned from the previous year and are already comfortable with each other. The new singer wonders, will the pack accept me? Will I ever become a part of them? Will they help me catch up?

Recently, a video appeared on social media showing a large herd of elk running. As they reached a well-traveled, straight, and open road, they met a barbed wire fence, which offered little challenge to the herd. The leader flew over the fence while cars stopped, one driver holding a video to capture the procession. Hundreds of elk cleared the fence with no resistance. One by one, sometimes several at a time, they leapt the barrier, moving toward pastures over the horizon. As the camera focused on this massive herd moving together, videographer and viewer alike began to notice a single animal—a bit smaller than many but not the smallest in the herd—unable to jump the barrier. The observers became fixated on the single elk. As more crossed, the animal began a frantic pace up and down the fence line, searching for a break in the wire. But there was none in sight. Fear and doubt were visible in the back and forth path.

Finally, the camera revealed success. With a decisive attempt, this last member of the herd cleared the hurdle. But focused solely on the fence, the camera had yet to document what met the elk on the other side of the road. The video was quite long and chronicled hundreds of animals. By the end of the video, the front of the herd must have been well over the next ridge, and it was impossible that the leader knew a member of his herd had almost been left behind. As the camera followed the final elk across the road, it was revealed that those bringing up the rear, though well off in the distance, were standing and waiting for this smaller, weaker member. Even when those in the lead could not see, members of the herd continued to look out for each other. Those bringing up the end of the impressive parade of elk refused to abandon even one member.

How can we, as educators, develop an atmosphere and culture in our programs in which the weak are not left behind, but instead encouraged, nurtured, and gathered into the fold? The atmosphere of the rehearsal classroom may by the single most important aspect of success for a choir. Without it, artistry and passion for text, harmonic structure, melody, and form cannot develop.

# CREATING A CULTURE OF SAFETY

Youth thrive when goals and expectations are high, clear, and attainable. In *Mentoring in the Ensemble Arts,*[1] Tim Sharp discusses leadership qualities from James Collins. "Leaders channel their ego needs away from themselves and into a larger goal of building a great organization." Taking this idea a step further within the classroom, setting the conductor's ego aside enables the focus to be properly placed on fostering a positive environment and realizing the needs of the singers while demonstrating an accepting, encouraging, and nurturing culture. Such an environment will enable a future of excellence and artistry.

In early years with a choir, the goals and expectations are the vision of the founder of the program. To achieve such a vision, it must become an integral part of the entire program, that which drives all projects and programming. (See Cincinnati Children's Choir Core Values in Appendix B.) Humans strive for excellence and acceptance. Therefore, when younger students see the level achieved by older students, they set that level as a goal for their own future. This is an example of peer pressure working in a positive way! Each year, the expectations of the ensemble will grow, surpassing the level of excellence set by those who came before, while simultaneously setting a new standard for future members.

Establish a zero tolerance policy for physical and emotional safety of each student, staff, parent, and volunteer/chaperone within strong music pedagogy and artistic instruction. Though it is imperative to start rehearsals by singing and making music—not going over policies and procedures, if it can at all be avoided—code of conduct expectations must be explained very early in the year and agreed to by every student and parent. (See examples of PARENT CODE OF CONDUCT and SINGER CODE OF CONDUCT in APPENDIX B.)

Anyone who has sung in a choir, been involved with youth sports, or even attended church knows that the culture of an organization is a mirror image of the person leading it. If the conductor demonstrates appreciation for guests in the room—whether observers, instrumentalists, or conductors—so will the ensemble. If the conductor demonstrates respect, acceptance, joy, and pride in the group, so will the ensemble. Encourage discussion about poetry, musical interpretation, and artistic presentation and welcome all responses. Validate each student's opinion, even as you gently steer the discussion toward your own musical interpretation. If the conductor demonstrates a commitment to and respect for the students and the ensemble, so will the ensemble be committed to and respectful of the conductor.

An extension of such a commitment comes in these words credited to Karen Bruno, a contributing author of this book. Help the singers see that they have "made a commitment to the people in this room—not to a time and a place but to each other." Understanding and experiencing that each singer is a valued and needed member of the entire group, choristers will deeply and emotionally commit to the ensemble, its staff, and leadership. Choir members will turn to each other for support through life's greatest challenges, heartbreaks, joys, and successes. They will welcome new members into the choir family, understanding that they are not only helping new singers feel welcome, they are continuing the culture from which they themselves have benefitted.

This being said, artistry will always trump personal friendships when it comes to ensemble commitment. In 2011, Eva Floyd, also a contributing author of this book, polled the advanced ensemble in the Cincinnati Children's Choir. A central question of the survey was, "What brings you back each week?" The options were as follows: 1) your friends and the desire to be together; 2) parents who insist on participation; or 3) the artistry achieved through your experience with the choir. Overwhelmingly, the students replied that artistry was the reason for their involvement. In spite of the fact that most members share membership with their closest friends from across three southwestern Ohio counties, Northern Kentucky, and southeastern Indiana, for over 95% of choir members, artistry is what brings them back every week.

# EXPLORING THE MUSIC THROUGH A CULTURE OF SAFETY

As conductors, we must understand why youth often prefer not to share in front of their peers. Much of the time, it is fear of failure: fear that others will not value his or her idea, talent, and/or interpretation. A culture of safety diminishes that fear and allows children and youth to openly explore the poetry and emotion contained in the music. The more input members have, the more they will feel ownership in the final product.

Self-evaluation and peer evaluation are invaluable tools in the choral classroom. Evaluating requires listening, knowledge based on past experience and teaching, and the ability to express it so others can benefit. When embedded in a safe environment, choristers will carefully choose their words, share what is going very well, and offer helpful criticism. Evaluation is always helpful during rehearsals, whether done individually, through one section evaluating another, or by individuals evaluating the entire ensemble. Individually, a concise way to gather their responses is to have them hold up, to their chest, a number of fingers. One finger is, "I blew it!" while five fingers expresses, "I nailed it!" This method can also help the conductor evaluate the volume of each singer, one being soft and five being loud. It can be used to answer any number of questions that the conductor will benefit from quickly knowing, while keeping the results between the singer and the director.

It is also very helpful to take time during rehearsal to have the choir evaluate themselves following a performance. The director may learn where they stumbled, as well as what knowledge the choir brought with them into the performance. Often, when a choir brings a lot of experience and knowledge into a performance, they find it difficult to step back and appreciate what they just accomplished. Like many conductors, they will continue to strive to make it better, to raise the bar. This is when the conductor can step in to help them sort out some of those thoughts, while guiding them to feel the pride in their accomplishment and their hard working attitude.

# OUTSIDE OF THE REHEARSAL ROOM

Providing opportunities for choir members to get to know each other outside of rehearsal will help to promote a welcoming atmosphere and safe place environment. This can be done through scheduled choir retreats, which should include rehearsal time, team-building activities, and food. Eating together and socializing in a relaxed environment—making sure that the leaders are reaching out to the newer, younger members—will lay a strong foundation that will transfer into the rehearsal room.

Traveling together also builds upon the environment of the ensemble. This can be a large tour, but that often comes at the end of a season and does not build upon the environment for the entire year. Exploring ways to collaborate with local or regional artists can serve the same purpose and avoid the high price tag of a trip (which may exclude members that do not have the resources to travel). It is often said, by conductors who are fortunate enough to collaborate with symphonies, the time in the holding room is as valuable as going on tour. Forced to be together in a confined space, working toward an exciting collaboration, enables the singers to get to know each other and creates a unified team through personal emotions, experience, and sharing. This, too, will transfer into performance. The responsibility of creating and maintaining a nurturing and productive environment lies with the director. Yet, once effectively achieved, it will self-perpetuate in many ways and the benefits to the ensemble will be immeasurable.

# THE REHEARSAL

## CHAPTER 2

# WARM-UPS

BY JOSHUA PEDDE

**W**arm-ups: the beginning of your rehearsal and the first sounds produced by your choir. When you think about how important these moments are, warm-ups become a very important part of the rehearsal in which directors and teachers set the mood of the rest of the rehearsal, work on tone, introduce new concepts, and so much more. When I was still a student and working with the Indianapolis Children's Choir, I was told by one of the directors that doing warm-ups was one of the most important parts of the rehearsal. Wow! Many people would not view the first minutes of rehearsal as the most exciting or influential, but hearing that made me stop and think. It changed my outlook on warm-ups and the attention that I needed to give to them.

So, why put so much time into warm-ups? First, the time devoted to warm-ups helps our singers to find focus and their "inner singer," as James Jordan said, or the "singer's spirit," as Weston Noble refers to it. It helps them leave behind the baggage of the day and prepare to create beautiful music. Second, it prepares the body/instrument for singing. Just as any athlete stretches and warms up before undertaking significant training or playing a game, we need to prepare our bodies for what is about to happen. Third, we teach healthy vocal technique during this time. Yes, we also teach through the music we rehearse and perform. However, here is a place in which to specifically focus on a technique your singers will use later. You are preparing the ensemble for what is about to happen! Fourth, you can build skills as an ensemble, including listening, tone, improvisation, and theory. And finally, you use this time to set the tone of the rehearsal. It allows you to build a safe environment in which your singers will feel comfortable singing and receiving feedback.

Before the choir ever sings a note, you must know what sound you are expecting them to create. I relate this to going on a road trip. Before you set out on the trip, you normally know your destination and how to get there. The same can be said for warm-ups. I am often asked about the sound of the choirs I work with and how it can be recreated. I tell them to do a lot of listening. Listen to groups that you respect and then practice how to recreate that sound in a healthy manner for yourself. In this digital age of Facebook and YouTube, you can easily listen to choirs from around the world and find vocal models to share, both good and bad. By listening, you will begin to refine the sound you want and how it can be recreated.

# AREAS OF FOCUS

We have established why it is important to devote time to warm-ups. Now it is time to talk about *what* to do during warm-ups. I am not going to give you specific exercises, but instead look at how to use warm-ups to create the best choral tone and an engaging, safe, and inclusive rehearsal environment.

First, no matter what tone you are trying to achieve, there are certain elements that must be present in everything you do. They are the following:

- Breath support

- Placement

- Intonation

- Resonance

- Vowel shapes

- Rhythmic unity

- Vocal expression

- Facial expression

I have taken all of these elements and placed them into five categories. These are the focus areas that I work to engage during the first few minutes of every rehearsal. All elements need to be working together to achieve the best choral sound!

- Breath: Breath is the foundation of singing. It is the fuel that powers our instrument. We want to use efficient and even breaths that create good tone.

- Soft Palate: We must maximize the space in our mouths by creating lift to help create resonance.

- Tongue: We must relax this muscle to eliminate tension in the throat and the jaw.

- Placement: Forward placement will help keep the tone pure, maximize resonance, and eliminate intonation issues. I tend to be brighter in my placement. I like it to sit right behind the sinus cavity in order to achieve resonance and ping.

- Lips: This creates vowel unification. A choir sounds its best when each singer's vowel shape is the same. Remember, keep those corners in and the lips relaxed. Often, directors say to have "round" lips, which can cause tension. Our goal is to have relaxed lips and when relaxed they should naturally be round without tension.

Is there one, correct way to do warm-ups? No. However, I like to keep the order to be consistent so that the singers have an anchor/routine in which to get engaged and focused at the beginning of the rehearsal. Here is my order:

- Physical/mental

- Breath

- Tone/vowels

- Range/flexibility

- Tuning

- Others, including diction/phrasing

## Physical

This is very literal. Any physical stretching will do. I even like to throw in something fun like tai chi or yoga to keep it interesting and to help bring relaxation into the rehearsal. I also insist that this portion be done in silence. This is where we begin to focus. As the director, you also have to remain silent. Don't give instructions or talk about the day or the upcoming rehearsal. There will be time for that later on. A few examples of physical warm-ups:

- Lift arms over head to expand ribcage and then move from side to side.

- Stretch (arms in front of body and behind, as well as shoulder, neck, and torso rolls).

- Give backrubs to other members of the choir (depending on age).

- Drop forward at the waist and hang limp, like a marionette; then lift up slowly, one vertebra at a time, until tall, aligned posture is achieved.

- Pull string from the top of your head.

- While taking slow, deep breaths, hold tai chi or yoga positions.

## Mental

This is something I use after stretching to begin to wake the singers up. I also love to throw these things into the middle of rehearsal while we are transitioning to keep them thinking. They are very simple games that are meant to keep the singer alert, as well as to make them laugh and have fun!

- Be My Mirror: This is like Simon Says. The singers must follow and do everything you do, including both movements and sounds.

- Yes/No game: The singers repeat a pattern of the words "yes" and "no," such as "yes, yes, no, no." Once the singers master this, then have them say the opposite of what you say. Anytime you say the word "yes," they say the word "no," and so on.

- Rhythmic Canon: Clap, pat, and/or stomp a pattern of four beats and have the singers echo the pattern back. Then begin to reduce the amount of time you rest from four beats to one beat.

- Memory Game (Solfege or Rhythmic): Place a melodic or rhythmic pattern on the board (even better if it is from a piece you are currently working on or about to introduce) and have the singers clap/say or sing it. Then begin to erase it, until the board is empty and they are repeating it from memory.

- Body Percussion: Similar to the rhythmic canon. You may also layer patterns over each other.

## Breath

Breathing is the battery of singing, and unfortunately, often the element that we skip in warm-ups. Take time to breathe and to teach proper breathing technique. By fixing this element you will save yourself time in the long run, because your singers will be producing a healthy and rich tone instead of a breathy, weak tone. We all have our favorite exercises. Below are some of mine:

- Raise arms and push air out on "sh"

- Breathe in for four beats and then out on "sh" or "ss"

- Breathe for four counts and then out on a rhythmic pattern

- Sixteen pulses beginning with quarter notes, then eighth notes, then triplets, then sixteenth notes on "ss" or "sh" or "vv"

- Rap a consonant pattern, such as "k-sh-b"

During each of these exercises, I like to have the singers place their hands on their diaphragms in order to make sure they are engaged, breathing low, and filling their entire lung capacity.

## Vowels

Now we reach the moment when the choir sings their first note, the time where you hear how their tone will be for that rehearsal. It is important that from the first moment they sing, you emphasize using good breath that only produces good tone. The breath is not escaping, allowing air to be heard in the tone (unless preparing for a specific genre of singing, such as jazz).

At the Indianapolis Children's Choir, we begin with a five-note pattern beginning on the C above middle C in F major and descending in step-wise motion to F. We repeat this pattern on the following vowels in the following order: oo, ee, eh, oh, and ah. This order is used because of the placement of the tongue. "Oo" relaxes the mouth. Then beginning with "ee," the tongue is high in the back of the mouth. With each successive vowel, the tongue begins to lower in position.

During the vowel exercise, we begin to work on creating space. Often times, directors say to imagine a space or object in your mouth. But if you place something in your mouth, what is your natural instinct? Swallow it! So if you are asking your singers to place this imaginary object or space in their mouth, they will swallow it. Instead, teach them about the soft palate, label it, and ask them to lift it and feel that sensation. (I find the soft palate by asking singers to run their tongues along the roofs of their mouths).

## Range

Next we work on expanding their range. We traditionally do "doo, bee, doo, bee, doo" beginning in F major. I like to play with the tempo while doing this, so no one can go on autopilot and everyone is forced to stay engaged. That is the issue with exercises that work range—they become repetitive and the singer zones out. When you find an exercise you like, look for ways to vary it using concepts such as tempo and diction.

## Phrasing

Phrasing can be worked on during all warm-ups, but often directors like to isolate this one element to achieve pure tone for a specific piece. If you do an exercise specifically for phrasing, I recommend using rounds. Rounds are a wonderful way for singers to listen to one another while singing something fun and engaging. Another exercise I like is singing an "ee" vowel starting on sol and sliding down to do and back to sol. This works on the legato line and also placement and range.

## Tuning

For tuning, I love to build chords. I like to begin on a unison pitch and move sections away from one another by half steps. I always keep one section on the beginning pitch. I like to explore several chord inversions, as well as augmented and diminished chords. This exercise keeps the singers ears engaged while they listen to both the voices within their section and the other sections as well. You can also do this exercise using solfege. You can either write the solfege ladder on the board or use hand signs. During all of this, continue to correct issues such as breath support, the soft palate, etc.

## Diction

We often focus all our time on creating beautiful vowels. However, if we also focus on the consonants it will help with tone placement and fix several technical issues. By having singers focus on the diction of the text, it will encourage them to place the sound forward and bring a brightness and resonance to the tone. A more forward-placed sound will bring clarity to the text. Remember, words are at the heart of what we do as singers. We must focus on their intelligibility so that the audience does not miss one second of the story or message we have to tell.

## Other Techniques

Between exercises, in order to release any tension that has begun, I like to do sirens or sighs to release the tension and relax the voice and also stretch the vocal folds. You can also use sighs and sirens to approach a note from above and then stop on that pitch. I often do this with higher pitches to help them tune.

I also love to echo back and forth with the choir. The art of echoing is fun and allows the director to adjust the sound of the choir by simply singing. I used this every day when I was teaching in my elementary music classroom. I took it into the choral rehearsal and had great success with it. Start simple. Sing a pattern to the choir and have them sing it back exactly. If it is not exact, sing it again until they repeat it correctly. Then move to a new pattern. This is also a great way to introduce and work on a new passage of music they may have difficulty with later in the rehearsal. I always start out simply with five notes and then build the phrase to make it more complex. I then change the length of the phrase and move the tonality around (again, to keep the singers engaged).

# ELEMENTS OF TEACHING

## Kinesthetic Movement

As humans, we always remember better when we add movement to whatever we are doing. It is natural for us to want to move and experience concepts. Singing follows this pattern. In our Western European culture, we do not naturally move while singing in a formal setting; however, watch any child, and you will sing them naturally move when they sing. We need to cultivate this and use it as we teach. Singers understand and retain musical concepts better when they actively experience them. Instead of talking about a musical concept, try doing a motion and experiencing the music in a new way! Then use these cues later as you work through your repertoire. A few examples of kinesthetic movements:

- Circles with fingers going forward = forward placement

- Large circles around chest = support

- Tapping fingers on palm of hand = short

- Throwing a Frisbee® = support and energy

- A flick = short and bright

- Pointing index fingers and moving forward = forward placement and phrasing

- Pointing at a single note = short

- Placing hands flat together = soft palate down

- Placing hands in circle shape = soft palate lifted

- Placing index fingers with space between them = vocal folds not meeting and air escaping

- Placing index fingers gently together = vocal folds meeting and air not escaping

## Singing Voice

Your choir is a vocal mirror of you. I know this is a difficult thing to read and take in. However, our choirs respond to us as directors and reflect that back to us. Modeling using your "best" singing voice is one of the most powerful and efficient ways to communicate a musical idea. Rather than talking about what you want, sing it! However, before you model it, you must make sure you model it correctly. It must be the way you want it to be sung. Also, remember that an operatic voice may not be the best choral voice. Always think about what is the best modeling voice. For men, the question of head voice or chest voice is always asked. My answer is, always use the best modeling voice. Just make sure it is relaxed and the sound you want. You can also use your singing voice to model two different examples and have the choir choose between them. You can do a "bad vs. good" or "A vs. B" example.

## Chanting Voice

If you are not confident in your singing voice or your voice is tired from a long rehearsal, use your chanting voice as a wonderful alternative. Because I work mainly with treble choirs, I have them chant in the head voice and not the chest voice. Chanting in this register replicates many of the sensations of singing and enables singers to experience new vocal techniques in a healthy way. Some of the benefits of using the chanting voice are:

- Balanced weight in the voice

- Unified vowels

- Smooth phrasing

- Connection between breath and sound

- Elimination of vocal tension

## Imagery/Metaphors

Singing is a physical activity that cannot be seen. Using imagery and metaphors help the singers create the tone for which we are listening. Choirs benefit from the use of words that describe both weight and color, such as light vs. heavy or bright vs. dark. By mixing weight and color we can achieve different tones. Examples would be:

- Sing that phrase a bright yellow, like that of a canary flying.

- Sing the opening as if you were carrying two heavy brown bags of groceries.

- Sing this as if it were a light white cloud floating across the sky.

You can also change the choral sound of a choir by accessing the sound found in their own minds. Using these images can achieve wonderful things. Examples would be:

- Sing like you are 23 years old.

- Sing like you are the best choir in the state.

- Sing as if you are the opera chorus at the Met.

Choirs can change their tone by simply accessing images and sounds in their minds. Remember, the choir is an image of you. If you sing dark, they sing dark. You sing bright, they sing bright.

## Other Things to Think About . . .

First, be sure to warm yourself up! You must be at the top of your game if you expect your choir to be at the top of theirs. Second, don't forget that a great sound starts at the beginning of the rehearsal, not when you begin your first piece of music. You must have the sound you want in your ear before the choir sings. Begin your warm-ups from the top down, not the bottom up. You want to cross over the break from the top.

What we (the directors) hear is not what they (the choir) hear! They must trust us. As in all relationships, trust is earned not given. You must earn their trust and in return they will create wonderful music for you. Always be honest with them, but always in a positive and respectful manner. Invite the choir members to lead and listen during warm-ups and in rehearsal. This will help you build trust within the ensemble because peers will be reinforcing what you are hearing on the podium.

Teach them everything in the music! Don't dumb it down. When I was teaching in the elementary school, I always taught the students everything. They knew what a soft palate was, and that to sing well it needed to be raised. They knew how the vocal folds worked and that tension was bad. Why do we think our singers cannot handle common terms that all professional musicians use? Regarding beginning singers versus advanced singers, my answer is always the same: good technique is good technique. Period. No matter whom you are teaching, they deserve and expect only the best training.

Do your warm-ups and rehearsals a cappella. Move away from the piano and trust yourself and your singers. The more you can get away from the piano, the more you will see your ensemble grow. Remember, only model for the choir, and don't sing with them. This is the time when your ears need to be open! You are there to listen and direct, not to be a member of the choir. Also, know your space from rehearsal room to performance hall. Work on your tone as if in the performance hall, not for the present rehearsal. Make the hall sing back to you!

## Take Warm-Ups (Rehearsals) to the Next Level

What can you do next? First, work outside your comfort zone! We all have our favorite warm-ups that we do week in and week out. But ask yourself, are they doing anything for your ensemble? Try new things. It is okay to fail! If you never try, you will never know! Tell the ensemble that you are doing something new and you want to see how it works. Take voice lessons and experiment with sound yourself. There is always something new to learn from another colleague. It takes time, but in the long run it will not only help you, but your ensemble as well. Invite in a guest that can model great sound, or colleagues who are wonderful conductors or singers. This will help expand the choir's sound library and give you more points of reference.

Study your scores and see what your singers are going to need from you. How can you prepare them better? Warm-ups are a great place to prepare those pitfalls that you see coming and can help to avoid them. Make sure you take time after each rehearsal to self-reflect either in your office, on the car ride home, or falling asleep after a long rehearsal. Keep evaluating your strengths and weaknesses and make changes in order to keep moving forward. Always know what you are doing, don't just go "off the cuff." You may do something you didn't intend and then have to work for a long time to correct it!

Finally, give the singers ownership of the product! The more ownership the ensemble has, the more they will give to the product. Remember that without them, there is no choir. They want to be part of the process and the more self-sufficient they become, the further you can move. Then you can turn your attention to new and finer details.

## CHAPTER 3

# REHEARSAL TECHNIQUES
## FOR DEVELOPING VOICES AND CHOIRS

BY SANDRA THORNTON

**M**ost collegiate music education majors are in awe of their collegiate choir directors and the artistry that they elicit from their singers. It is magical how these directors are able to bring a group of college students with varying backgrounds together in a room and, in a few short minutes, create a cohesive, unified, and beautiful sound. Inspired and working toward becoming a conductor, most of these students attend rehearsal with the intent of absorbing every nuance of Brahms, Haydn, and Bach that comes from the director's baton, confident that they will be imparting this knowledge to a choir of their own some day.

However, for many of these new collegiate graduates, the dream of conducting varsity level choirs at a "double A" high school with a substantial working budget is not typically something that happens in their first teaching position. More often than not, the reality of the situation that they find themselves in is the complete opposite and many new teachers find themselves working in programs where the students are just beginning their musical training. To say that this new position is challenging is an understatement!

It's easy to walk into a new position fully expecting the students to be able to sing high quality, age-appropriate repertoire with a beautiful and open choral tone and attention to all of the wonderful articulations that bring the music to life, since that's what these former college students experienced during their own collegiate training. However, this is not always the case and, many times, the biggest struggle for a teacher working with beginning vocal ensembles is not creating beautiful conducting gestures, but finding ways of helping these students to match pitch and work toward elemental unison singing.

If beginning singers are to be able to have a successful experience in the classroom, teachers are going to have to stop expecting that these students can just *do* whatever is expected of them and *teach* them *how* to do it. Whether a seasoned veteran or brand new to the trade, one of the biggest, yet most rewarding challenges for a choir director is structuring a successful rehearsal made up of developing singers. Experiences based in solid vocal and musical training are the foundation of everything to come in their choral lives.

When working with younger singers, there are some inherent challenges that directors need to keep in mind. Often, this may be the first experience in a musical setting for these developing singers. Additionally, the younger the ages of the singers in the ensemble, the shorter the educator may find the singers' attention spans. Literacy is also an issue with many beginning singers, and developing music literacy will be key to growing independent musicians. Finally, children need kinesthetic experiences taught to them through play. The engagement of their creative spirit is imperative in creating a positive, nurturing environment in which they can learn and grow.

## FIRST EXPERIENCE IN A MUSICAL SETTING

Many students in beginning ensembles are experiencing their first organized choral setting. This experience is an introduction to a lifelong love of singing and choral music. Often times, inexperienced singers are shy. They may sing all the time at home and feel comfortable doing so in front of family or friends, yet feel nervous about having to do so in front of their new peers. Apprehension of the unknown can also be a contributing factor to behavioral choices in these first few rehearsals. Therefore, it is important to focus on building an environment that makes each singer feel safe, comfortable, and valued as a person. Creating such a classroom culture of acceptance is essential and one of the main tenants of the Cincinnati Children's Choir philosophy. If we build a safe place for the child to enter, they feel comfortable opening themselves socially, emotionally, and physically.

Welcoming each singer at the door as they enter each rehearsal, learning their names in the first few weeks of a new season, attempting to learn bits of information about them, and demonstrating a personal interest are strategies that must be sincere (children know the difference) and employed from the start. Choristers should also be encouraged to get to know others around them. Communication from singer to singer and between director and singer is key to building an ensemble that trusts each other and trusts the director. It is much easier to go into a new situation and feel comfortable expressing yourself if the support system surrounding you, your group, and your director is evident. The ultimate goal is for singers to feel comfortable expressing themselves expressively and vocally, so that directors can help them expand as young musicians.

Newcomers entering a rehearsal space are entering the unknown, especially when participating in a community choral program. In school, students abide by a specific set of expectations and procedures that are established in core curriculum classes. But the expectations of successful membership in a community choral organization may be new territory. It is the director's responsibility to set clear expectations and create a culture of acceptance, learning, and artistry that comfortably bridges the gap between what they enter knowing and what they will grow to be as a choir.

The atmosphere should be set on the first day and then reinforced throughout each subsequent rehearsal. Making music is the main reason for being together, so much of the reinforcement of procedures and expectations needs to be done while rehearsing and experiencing choral artistry. Establishing such standards will help to pace each rehearsal to come while engaging students from the start, thus avoiding long lectures, holding their attention, and accomplishing tasks quickly.

Begin rehearsals with a "brain warm up"—a game or activity that brings the singers together mentally and helps the singers create an atmosphere in which they are ready to make music. Then use the transitions between activities to integrate small chunks of procedural information such as:

- How to enter the rehearsal space

- Bathroom procedures

- How to answer or ask questions during the rehearsal

- What to do if you need a drink during the rehearsal

- How to exit the rehearsal space

Constantly reinforce good behavior, rehearsal procedures, and singing technique as the choir transitions from one activity to the next.

# SHORTER ATTENTION SPANS

When working with teenagers and adults, choir directors can spend a good deal of time on a single piece of music, reinforcing the concepts that the singers are to assimilate. With younger singers, that type of detail work can still take place, as younger singers don't tend to overthink like adults do, but it has to be done in a different way, because their attention spans are shorter than that of adults.

When working with beginning choirs, the younger the singer, the shorter the attention span, which is a concept that many directors can find a bit daunting. It is important that time is structured in such a way that singers are successful in accomplishing the goals of the rehearsal while still remaining engaged in the learning process. Therefore, varying the stimulus quickly and often is key. Our youngest singers in the Cincinnati Children's Choir typically have an attention span of eight to ten minutes on a given subject, which is not a lot of time. Activities need to be well thought out and swiftly paced, while structured in such a way that all learning styles are included.

Learning activities that encompass many different methodologies, such as Orff Schulwerk, Kodály, and Dalcroze, need to be incorporated into the lesson so that each child can be reached in his or her own learning style. Structuring lessons around Gardner's theory of multiple intelligences, developed by Howard Gardner in his 1983 book *Frames of Mind: The Theory of Multiple Intelligences,*[1] is also helpful in ensuring success for all singers. According to Gardner, there are seven distinct types of intelligences:

- Visual-Spatial: These students think in terms of visual space, like architects and sailors. They are very aware of their environments and like to draw, construct puzzles, and daydream. These students "think in pictures" and often remember things by associating a visual picture to the concept.

- Bodily-Kinesthetic: These students have a keen sense of body awareness and often use their bodies to reinforce what they are saying or doing. They like movement, hands on learning, acting and role-play. Bodily-kinesthetic thinkers communicate well through body language and are easily taught through physical activity.

- Musical: These students show sensitivity to rhythm and sound. They love music, but are also sensitive to sounds in their environment and may study better with music in the background. They can be taught by turning lessons into lyrics, speaking rhythmically, and tapping out time.

- Interpersonal: These students have a keen talent for understanding and interacting with others. They learn best by interacting with others and have a strong sense of empathy and "street smarts." Students who are interpersonal learners often learn best through group activities and dialogues.

- Intrapersonal: These independent learners tend to be very in tune with their own inner feelings. They have wisdom, intuition, and motivation, as well as strong will, confidence, and opinions and are often taught through independent study and introspection.

- Linguistic: These learners have highly developed auditory skills and often think in words. They like reading, word games, and making up poetry or stories. They can be taught by encouraging them to say and see words and to read text together.

- Logical-Mathematical: These learners think abstractly and conceptually. They are easily able to see and explore patterns and relationships. They like to experiment, solve puzzles, and ask cosmic questions. They are best taught through logic games and investigations.

Most students will possess qualities of a combination of these multiple intelligences to varying degrees, so it is important to use multiple methods of teaching the same concept in order to promote maximum retention. For example, in introducing ideas like "crescendo" and "decrescendo," a few activities can be done in quick succession in order to both introduce and allow the singers to experience the concept:

- As younger singers gain more success through the idea of "sound before symbol," a simple rote melody song, such as the first phrase of "Twinkle, Twinkle, Little Star", that includes a crescendo in the first sub-phrase ("Twinkle, twinkle, little star . . .") and a decrescendo in the second sub-phrase ("How I wonder what you are . . .") will allow them to experience these dynamic concepts first before delving into what they are and how they are produced. This activity appeals to both the musical learners and the logical-mathematical learners, as the singers are experiencing the relationship between the two dynamic shifts.

- Singers can also locate the two symbols in a piece of music and describe what they look like. Most of the time, younger singers will describe a crescendo as an angle that goes from small to big, which describes the sound moving from small/quiet to big/loud. Older singers may describe them in the mathematical terms of "greater than" or "less than" signs, which also work in music. These "location" and "description" methods will appeal to visual-spatial and linguistic learners, who often need to associate symbols with pictures and verbally describe what they look like.

- You may also allow the students to move in a way that shows how a crescendo and decrescendo function. This can be done using phrases in the choir music or in the original "Twinkle, Twinkle, Little Star" song. A simple sweeping of the hand up or down to show a crescendo or decrescendo, or an actual movement of the body from a seated position to a standing position and vice versa would also allow bodily-kinesthetic oriented learners an opportunity to physically show these musical concepts.

These activities should take around five to eight minutes total. With swift pacing and quick transitions, even the youngest singers should be able to assimilate these concepts into their musical vocabulary. In quick succession, the singers can experience these concepts by showing them with their body, putting them into their singing voice, applying them to a piece of music, and by describing both what they look like and what they do. In that way, the concept is being presented in multiple ways at a pace that corresponds with their attention spans. The concept of "crescendo" and "decrescendo" may need to be reviewed with these developing singers from time to time, but they now have the building blocks to start associating them with musical examples in other pieces of their repertoire.

## MUSICAL LITERACY

For students in developing choirs, musical literacy is a key factor in their overall success. Students joining beginning choirs are at a point in their schooling where they are just learning how to read and, for these singers, even reading the text to the chosen repertoire can be a struggle. Directors should not assume that these singers have the knowledge and literacy skills needed to be instantly successful at following a choral octavo. The nuance of following a musical score needs to be taught. Most singers, unless they've had prior musical training, will be new to observing things like systems and measures, so directors cannot expect them to follow the up and down motion of the notes of their vocal line if they have no idea where in the music to look to find their specific part. Once singers know how to follow a score, they can begin to get into the specifics of literacy.

As mentioned above, the idea of "sound before symbol" becomes crucial in working with these developing singers. Singing music is a visceral act and children need to experience the nuances of pitch, rhythm, and articulation before they can be expected to incorporate them into their knowledge base. At this stage, rote-based learning experiences help guide the learning process. Singers remember the concept by recreating the initial experience through repetition of the performance of the concept. Once the concept is ingrained, the musical symbols can be slowly introduced, expanding the developing singer's musical vocabulary.

Working with young singers does not have to be a daunting task. When structured in certain ways, rehearsals with developing ensembles are some of the most fun and rewarding experiences of music making, because of the excitement embodied by this particular age group. There is a vitality that surrounds children when they are first experiencing new things and it's exciting when that new experience happens to be music! For our newest singers, singing music needs to be something that they can gravitate to and find pleasure in right away.

Imagery, role-play, and body motion can be used in rehearsal all the time. By gauging the body language of the singers, the director can assess when to push farther and when to move to the next activity. Singers will let you know, in not so many words, when they are really getting a lot out of a particular activity and when it is time to switch gears.

## MOVEMENT IN REHEARSAL

Because they are still so young and new to this, movement is crucial during rehearsals. Young singers need to move frequently. This may include specified motions in each warm-up activity (altering between sitting, standing and stretching), walking/stomping/patting/clapping/tapping to the steady beat, and encouraging singers to move their arms/hands/heads/legs/feet in a way that describes the music. The positive outcome is two-fold: singers start to feel free to incorporate those movements into their sound, and thus free up a lot of vocal tension that comes from having to hold the body in a rigid fashion while singing. The music becomes an organic experience that incorporates both their voices and their bodies. They get into the music that they are performing and are much more engaged in creating artistry than if they were still.

Additionally, moving also helps to improve their attention spans. More and more, students at increasingly earlier grades are being expected to go longer periods in school sitting still and being quiet. By the time they get out of school for the day, they are full of the pent-up energy that is inherent to being a child. They need an outlet to healthily expend that energy! If given an opportunity to move, children are able to work out all of that nervous energy that gets in the way of their focus abilities. It creates a situation where they are actually able to focus for larger periods of time because they have been given the opportunity to free up their bodies.

# ROLE-PLAY—"WRONG WAY" VS. "RIGHT WAY"

Pretend playing while singing is the basis of much of the rehearsal time in the Cincinnati Children's Choir. Oftentimes, this is done in terms of extremes—such as having younger singers oscillate between exaggeratedly singing a warm-up or line of their repertoire the "wrong way" (pinched tone with a lowered soft palate and flat vowels) and the "right way." At this point in their musical lives, the physical sensation that they experience while singing correctly is the main teaching tool for them. Directors can explain about a lifted soft palate, open sound, and tall vowels, but it means nothing to them unless they can physically experience what that actually feels like. Once singers experience the feeling of an open tone and correct vowel placement, that feeling can be recreated.

In terms of role-play, creating warm-ups or singing the music as though the singers are characters in the actual music itself is something that helps to free up the vocal sound. The character can come from just about anywhere and embrace a multitude of emotions: happy, sad, scared, excited, tired, nervous, and/or elated. This changes up the way the sound is produced, affects the amount of breath support the choristers sing with, and alters the overall tone quality of the choral sound. It's a great way to get the choristers experimenting with their singing voice in a way that is free play for them.

# IMAGERY IN THE MUSIC

Throughout rehearsal, use imagery to describe and discuss the story of the music. This helps the singers to develop a sense of ownership of the repertoire, especially if they are the ones telling the story of what is going on both in the text and in the music itself. It also lends itself to some beautiful musical moments that might not have been there if these types of conversations didn't take place.

Storytelling and questioning techniques led by the director can lead the singers to the message of the particular song on which they are working. More often than not, when given the opportunity, singers describe what's happening in the music and how it makes them feel far better than it being dictated to them via the director. When those ideas are put into their musical sound, some incredible life and excitement starts to infuse the music.

# MUSIC GAMES

Throughout the course of each rehearsal, musical games can be an integral part of building up musical skills and keeping the momentum of the rehearsal flowing. Starting each rehearsal with a mental or focus game gets each singer in the right frame of mind to make music for the next hour or more.

## Step Behind

In this game, start off by doing a basic motion that your students do with you, such as placing your hands on your head, touching your nose, placing your hands on your hips, touching your toes, etc. Once they have the hang of it, add another layer of challenge by having them do each motion "one step behind" you. Essentially, you are doing a "movement round" in which you are group one and they are group two. If you want to add an additional layer to the experience, break them into two or more groups and have a leader (either you or a student) begin the motions, while the first group follows the leader and the second group follows the first group. In the Cincinnati Children's Choir, we typically start off by moving at about 50 or 60 beats per minute, but the tempo can grow to increase the challenge level.

## Poison Rhythm

This game is good to use after singers have learned the basics of Kodály-based rhythm (quarter note equaling "ta" and eighth notes equaling "ti-ti," etc.). For this game, begin by writing a basic one-measure rhythm on the board. For the beginning ensembles, I stick with one measure of common time. We go over how we would speak it and then we clap it. This rhythm now becomes the "poison". Each singer stands and the director claps a series of one-measure rhythms that the singers clap back. If, at any time, the director claps the "poison" rhythm and a singer claps it back, that singer is "out" and has to sit down. The longer the game goes on, the more the director tries to stump the remaining standing singers by clapping rhythms that are similar to the "poison" rhythm and increasing the tempi of the examples. This is a great way to incorporate rhythmic notation literacy into the rehearsal plan. Specific rhythmic examples from the songs being performed can also be used in this game to reinforce what is happening in the music.

## Telephone

This game takes a bit of time, but is great for aural memory and solfege usage. It is a good game to use when the singers have experience using solfege and Curwen hand signs. The director takes a brief melodic figure from a piece of music that the choir is working on (or just makes up a melodic phrase) and sings it quietly on solfege into the ear of the person at the end of the first row. The person then sings it into the ear of the person next to him or her until the melody snakes its way around to the last person in the choir. That person then sings it into the ear of the choir director and the director sings it out loud for everyone to hear. It's interesting for the singers to see if and how the melody alters as it's being passed around. Another layer to add to this game would be to sing multiple melodies, one for each row that harmonize with each other and see if they end up the same when they make it to the end of the row, having each row sing their melody together once they're done.

### Rhythm Sentences

Though this isn't a game, it is a good way to aurally, kinesthetically, and visually show and perform different rhythms, incorporating both small and large groups of singers. The director starts out by bringing together four or more singers in the front of the room and having them stand like different notational figures:

- One singer with their hands clasped above their head represents a quarter note (ta).

- Two or more singers with their left hand placed on their neighbor's right shoulder represent eighth notes (ti-ti).

- Two singers holding hands represent half notes (ta-a).

- Three singers holding hands represent dotted half notes (ta-a-a).

- Four singers holding hands represent whole notes (ta-a-a-a).

- Any singers with their hands over their mouths (either alone or holding hands) represent quarter or half rests.

The rest of the choir then "reads" the rhythms that their peers are creating by reading from left to right while clapping the rhythm that they see. A way to add another layer would be to encourage the demonstrating students to come up with their own rhythm. You may also break the choir into small groups and have them "read" each other's rhythm sentences.

# POSITIVE REINFORCEMENT

A large part of structuring a successful rehearsal with developing choirs is having a strong sense of rehearsal management. Pacing throughout rehearsal activities will help keep their attention on the flow of the rehearsal, as will establishing a behavior plan that includes consistent positive reinforcement.

With young singers, it's much easier to adjust their behavior, when necessary, by observing all of the things that they're doing right as opposed to doing wrong. By publicly acknowledging a singer who is standing with correct singing posture or efficiently getting the next piece of music out, other singers learn what is acceptable in a rehearsal setting. A simple comment such as, "I really like how fast row two got out their scores and are quietly looking at me, ready to go" goes a lot farther with beginning singers than, "Everyone be quiet so that we can move on to the next piece of music." By choosing to comment on a behavior that the singers should emulate instead of negatively commenting on a behavior that is disruptive, expectations to the singers are relayed in a positive and loving manner.

Given the nature of younger singers, however, sometimes behavior disruptions need be addressed in a more immediate manner. In those cases when the behavior can't be adjusted by other positive behavior support methods, be as direct as possible and tell the singer specifically what the group needs to be doing so that everyone can be successful. For instance, if a singer is habitually speaking out without being called on in rehearsal and it is becoming a disruption, the director may say, "We raise our hands and wait to be called on if we have something to share." It is a more direct approach, but still allows the singer in question to feel respected and valued.

All in all, a developing choir of younger singers is one of the most rewarding ensembles with which to work, due largely to the fact that every musical experience that we provide for them is new and exciting. It is our training ensembles that have some of the biggest potential for vocal growth and, as choir directors, we have an amazing opportunity to open up a brand new world for these singers—a world where they can feel accepted, supported, valued, and talented. By teaching our developing singers the fundamentals of what being in a choir is all about and how to be a successful contributor, these singers become our strongest assets, both in their training ensembles and down the line in more advanced ensembles. If given the tools and materials to be successful, these young singers will grow into the singers that populate our advanced choirs, eventually becoming adults that continue to value singing and are supporters of the arts in our communities.

CHAPTER 4

# ORFF SCHULWERK IN THE CHORAL SETTING

BY ROBYN LANA

The training and experiences to which a teacher is exposed usually form a philosophy for the style and process of their teaching career. Experiences in Orff Schulwerk—in which the learner explores, creates, and strengthens musicianship skills through instruments, song, speech, drama, and movement—can prompt an educator to think outside the box when teaching and presenting material to singers of all ages.

One of the strongest tools in an Orff Schulwerk classroom is play. Children learn through play. Creating, sharing, exploring, smiling, and laughing are attributes of a classroom environment in which the children feel safe enough to share their creative ideas and interpretations. Imagine expanding that teaching style to include middle school singers who explore text and express poetry through their imaginations and life experiences, and then bring that expressiveness into a choral performance. Imagine youth choirs comfortably and confidently moving to and interpreting not just the sound of a recorded ensemble, but their own music as they rehearse. By internalizing and connecting to the music on an instinctual level, they will find ownership of the final product.

In the years after World War I, Carl Orff created a process of teaching music through movement and playing modest instruments. The Bavarian society in which he lived was a singing culture and to supplement that experience, he created barred instruments and borrowed simple percussion instruments from Asia, Africa, and South America. He encouraged his students to *experience* the music—feeling phrases, note values, and artistry in the music. This personal experience led his students to improvise and create their own music. Gunild Keetman, a colleague of Orff who spent her life disseminating their shared work in music education, said that Orff "did much not only to tell, but also to show, the effectiveness and artistry of the Schulwerk approach."[1]

The rise of the Socialist Party in 1933 Germany stifled the work of Orff and his colleagues. Access to institutions and experts came to an abrupt stop across the region. In 1936, Orff was asked to compose opening music for the Berlin Olympics, resulting in an international stage for his work. Though not truly representative of the Schulwerk approach and the creativity that was inherently part of the experience, the ceremonies showed thousands of children playing instruments and dancing, and in turn drew attention to Orff Schulwerk and its benefits. Over a decade later, he was asked to expand his teaching method for younger children. Across all ages, his approach emphasizes the common skill of singing. At a later age comes playing instruments, drama and text exploration, movement, and improvising.

In *Orff Schulwerk: Reflections and Directions*,[2] Cecelia Wang reviews elements of brain-based learning from the work of Caine and Caine. Key principles related to the choral classroom are:

- People innately search for meaning. In the choral classroom, that corresponds with finding repertoire of musical, cultural, historical, and poetic value.

- When people express, the learning is deeper and more personal. When singers are able to relate to and express the text and artistry within a composition, they experience a connection to the music that is deeper than observation, rote learning, or technical correctness in the performance.

- Learning must be focused, though individuals must always be fully aware of what is happening around them. Chorally, that includes performing as an ensemble with blend, singing harmony in multiple parts as well as accompanying instrumentation, and accounting for acoustics and the setting in which the rehearsal or performance is taking place.

- Learning is social. Singing in a choir requires sharing the most personal instrument created with those around you, and interacting with members of the choir, the director, and the accompanist as a team.

- Challenges heighten learning while threats obstruct learning. As explored in CHAPTER ONE: THE ENVIRONMENT, creating a safe place where all are welcomed will strengthen learning and the ability to share, express, and perform at potential.

Understanding the process, sequence of learning, and philosophies of Orff Schulwerk are essential to implementing the Schulwerk approach into the choral classroom. In addition to certification and teacher training workshops, here are several suggested print resources:

*Discovering Orff: A Curriculum for Music Teachers* by Jane Frazee with Kent Kreuter

*Discovering Keetman* by Jane Frazee

*Orff Schulwerk: Reflections and Directions* by Cecilia Wang

*Orff Re-Echoes, Book II: Selections from the Orff Echo and the Supplements* by Isabel McNeill Carley

*The Crooked River Choral Project* (Various)

To begin applying, choose repertoire that has musical, poetic, historical, and educational value. Once you have assessed the value of the music chosen, a path for presenting each piece at the readiness level of the singers can be determined.

# INCORPORATING DRAMA TO EXPLORE THE TEXT

Puppets can be used to introduce the story of the music. For example, "The Wise Old Owl"[3] by Cynthia Gray uses the following children's poem:

> The wise old owl sat in an oak.
>
> The more he heard, the less he spoke.
>
> The less he spoke, the more he heard.
>
> Why aren't we all like that wise old bird?
>
> Why aren't we more like the bird?

Using a puppet with arms and hands that can be controlled by the adult, a melody can be introduced by the teacher. While the teacher sings, the puppet demonstrates the following movements:

"The wise old owl sat in an oak"

"The more he heard"

"The less he spoke."

"Why aren't we all like that wise old bird?
Why aren't we more like the bird?"

The children then imitate the movements while the teacher sings again. Having heard the tune twice and mirrored motions that reflect the poetry, most elementary children will be able to sing the melody correctly. Younger children or children not accustomed to such activities may benefit from practice echoing phrases and movements beforehand.

This activity may be extended by adding barred instruments to Cynthia Gray's piece, as follows:

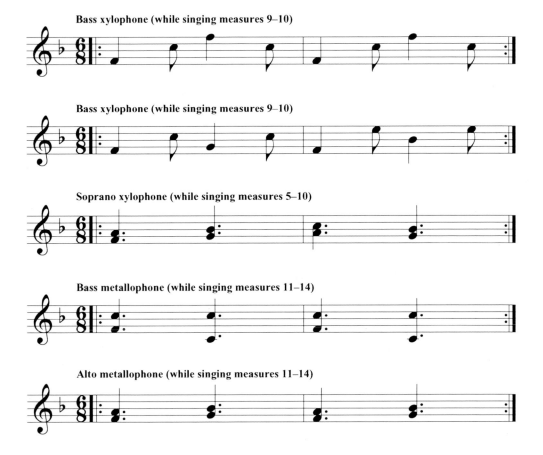

# INCORPORATING MOVEMENT

Movement helps to internalize many elements of music, and students of any age will benefit from kinesthetic connections to repertoire and elements of music. Movement can be integrated into sight-reading activities, as well as ostinatos and partner songs. When an educator can introduce creative ways to move to the written score, students will often have more success learning their part. An excellent example of this can be found in "I'm Gonna Sing When the Spirit Says Sing,"[4] arranged by Rochelle Mann and C. Scott Hagler. The setting is for SSA and uses a countermelody and a vocal ostinato to accompany the melody line.

In this setting, the opening is a unison countermelody:

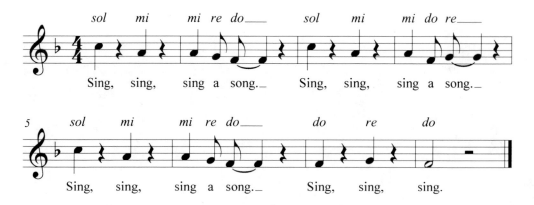

To introduce the countermelody, have the children echo while using solfege and Curwen hand signs. Show the students the following staff:

Ask them to identify the key signature and the home tone of DO. Point out other syllables on the scale, and then sing and echo random combinations using both solfege and Curwen hand signs. Within the random combinations, include the phrases of the countermelody. Once the children are comfortable exploring different solfege patterns, hand out the printed score. Ask them what they recognize about the music. Then read the music using hand signs. Ask them if it is familiar. Most will recognize it as the countermelody that has already been explored. When the countermelody is comfortable, sing the melody along with them as a duet.

Repeat the process with the ostinato that appears later in the score:

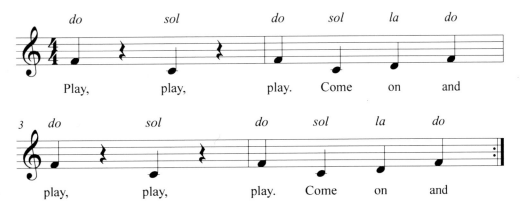

Finally, teach the melody to the entire group (this should be taught last). Then, incorporate movement. Split the group into three even groups. Give the countermelody group scarves and ask them to create a "scarf dance" for their part. It is helpful to refer to the scarf (and not the student) as the one doing the dancing, as it relieves anxious students of the pressure of having to perform movement in front of their peers.

Ask the ostinato group (altos) to create a clapping pattern/body percussion pattern for their part. If students are unsure, demonstrate an eight-beat pattern: clap right hands (play), together (rest), left (play), together (rest), both (play), together (come), patsch (on), together (and). Then have each pair of partners create their own pattern.

Ask the melody group to create movement that reflects the words they are singing. Once each group has had time to develop their movements and demonstrate them for the class, lead the ensemble through the printed score, bringing in each group as indicated. Prepare them for a cue that will indicate whether they should all sing the melody or a combination of different parts. It is helpful to have the words of the melody written on the board in front of the group, so that they know which verse they are singing, as there are four verses with slight variations.

This octavo also presents a perfect opportunity to incorporate ostinati on barred instruments. If done strictly as a classroom activity, the piece may stay in F major. If performed for an audience, instruments should be added after the modulation to G major. In an appropriate setting—perhaps an informance—use all of the movement in addition to the instrument parts, as an opportunity to educate parents and administrators about the learning process that occurs in the choral or singing classroom.

## CHAPTER 5

# KODÁLY IN THE CHORAL SETTING

BY EVA FLOYD

The Kodály method of teaching music is a Hungarian approach to music education that begins in kindergarten and continues through professional training at teacher colleges and the Liszt Academy. Zoltan Kodály (1882–1967) was a leading figure in Hungarian music education in the early- and mid-twentieth century. Together with his colleagues and students, he developed a national system of music education in Hungary based on sequential pedagogical principles using Hungarian folksongs. After the success of the International Society for Music Education conference held in Budapest in 1964, foreign music teachers labeled this Hungarian approach to music education the "Kodály method." The essence of this approach to music education is more than a method, toolbox, or sequence of steps. It is a comprehensive philosophy that permeates every musical lesson, rehearsal, and classroom in Hungary.

Kodály himself did not write a specific philosophy per se; however, his philosophy is evident in his various writings and in the actions of the Hungarian teachers. He believed that students should be taught to think musically—to think in sound. This can also be described as *inner-hearing,* which is the purposeful process of hearing music mentally in the absence of physical sound,[1] or by the term "audiating" as described by Edwin Gordon: "When we are hearing in our minds music for which the sound is no longer or never has been physically present."[2] This skill is monitored and developed by teachers in various ways, but most frequently by singing. Kodály believed that music education should be based on singing: "If one were to attempt to express the essence of this education in one word, it could only be: singing."[3] Hungarian teachers believe singing to be the most efficient way of developing the inner ear, and that singing is both a prerequisite and concurrent activity to instrumental study. The idea that singing develops one's internal hearing is important in the Kodály concept of music education because singing activities lay the foundatation for notational understanding. This type of experiential-based learning is also known as "rote before note" or "sound before sign." This idea of education was expressed by theorist Johann Heinrich Pestalozzi (1746–1827) and is not new or isolated to the Kodály approach alone, but rather a basic idea of effective teaching, applied to a musical context.

Music teachers in North America have adapted this approach to music education in general music classrooms by employing a preparation, presentation, and practice sequence of instruction.[4] Physical, aural, and visual preparation elements are embedded in the lessons and activities, which contain the musical element that will be presented to the students. The teacher isolates the rhythmic or melodic element from the activity and presents this concept to the students. In this stage of presentation the teacher transfers responsibility to the students—they take ownership of this concept in name, notation, and sound, which is now in their consciousness. Immediately following presentation, the teacher provides activities in which the students can practice the new musical concept in a variety of contexts (examples include reading, writing, part-work, improvisation, and listening). The musical element is now part of the students' inner-hearing vocabulary and will be reinforced with multiple opportunities for practice.

This process of systematically teaching new music elements is very effective when applied to a group of students over time, ideally from kindergarten through university. When working with a community choral group, the level of internal music understanding varies greatly among the singers. They do not come to the ensemble with a standard level of preparation because they all come from different schools and teachers. This creates an uneven musical ensemble. In these situations, the preparation-presentation-practice process requires adaptation for the specific musical situation at hand, while the overall goal remains the same: to help students develop their musical thinking and internal musical vocabulary (inner-hearing/audiation) while learning to perform quality choral music.

# REHEARSAL TOOLS

Kodály did not invent solfege pitch syllables; rather, he drew from the work of previous pedagogues such as Guido of Arezzo, Sara Glover, and John Curwen, who created and adapted pitch syllables and hand signs to enhance music teaching and learning. Kodály used movable do with a la-based minor solfege system as a tool to help students internally organize sound. The solfege syllables help singers recall how the pitches relate to each other, and it is important for teachers to use the syllables purposefully with this goal in mind. Teaching students that the half steps are between mi-fa and ti-do are the key to success when using solfege syllables.

Using solfege syllables in rehearsal helps singers understand pitch in its tonal context. Kodály spoke of its benefits with his students: "In my folk music lessons at the Liszt Academy, I found that if a student sang a folk tune with text, and it was with insecurity or bad intonation, afterwards when he sang it with sol-fa, it was crystal-clear, as if it wasn't the same student. Why? Because for every single sound he had to make conscious its role in the given tonality."[5]

Students may be very curious about the syllables themselves, where they came from, and why they are the way they are. Sharing the chant "Ut Queant Laxis" with your students, as either a singing experience or simply as a listening experience, will help give students a historical understanding of the syllables and help them to better understand the purpose for using the syllables. Students may be curious to know that "do" was originally "ut," and that this chant only used six pitches (hexachord). When eventually expanded to a full diatonic scale, the seventh degree was originally called "si" (Glover used "ti").

## Ut Queant Laxis (Hymn to St. John the Baptist)

Guido of Arezzo (circa 991–1033)

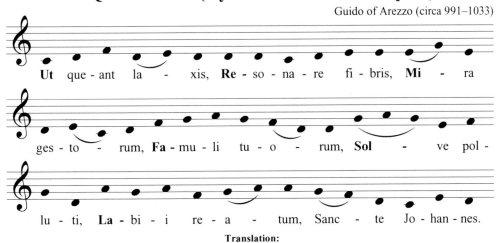

Ut que - ant la - xis, **Re** - so - na - re fi - bris, **Mi** - ra
ges - to - rum, **Fa** - mu - li tu - o - rum, **Sol** - ve pol -
lu - ti, **La** - bi - i re - a - tum, Sanc - te Jo - han - nes.

**Translation:**
So that your servants may, with loosened voices, resound the wonders,
of your deeds, clean the guilt, from our stained lips, Saint John.

Syllables can be altered to reflect chromatic changes in pitch. The vowel sounds are brightened with a sharp and darkened with a flat. Sharpened examples include, do-di, re-ri, fa-fi, sol-si, and la-li (mi and ti already imply a half-step relationship to the pitch above). Flattened examples include ti-te, la-le, sol-se, mi-me, and re-ra (do and fa already imply a half-step relationship to the pitch below). Sometimes you will hear teachers flatten vowels with [ɑ] alterations such as ti-ta, la-lo, sol-sa, mi-ma, and re-ra. It is the same concept as before, simply using a different vowel (see below).

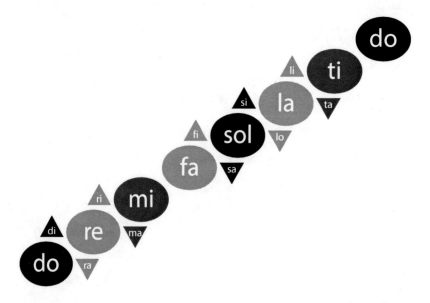

La-based minor is successful with helping students internalize and accurately perform in minor. Teachers often resist the idea because of previous experience with do-based minor, but students easily understand the idea when it is presented effectively. Any solfege syllable can be tonic, or a resting note, just as "Ut Quaent Laxis" used re as the resting tone in the dorian mode. It is important to remember the half-step relationships of ti-do (and later mi-fa) in the minor mode, as this creates the melodic scale formula for the ear. Knowing this makes it easier to understand the half-step/whole-step formula for building scales. The key to success with la-based minor is that the known syllables represent aurally where whole steps and half steps occur. No alternations are needed to hear and understand the character of natural minor. Later, it is easy to sing melodic and harmonic minor once the flavor of minor is firmly established. This is also true for singing in modes with re, me, fa, and sol as resting tones, as in the Dorian, Phrygian, Mixolydian, and Lydian modes, respectively.

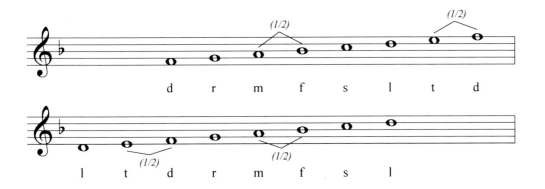

d r m f s l t d

l t d r m f s l

Using Curwen hand signs with solfege syllables helps students to kinesthetically reinforce relationships between pitches. The hand signs should reflect the spatial distances between pitches vertically and give a visual character to each sound. Teachers can alter the hand signs for chromatic adjustments by lifting a finger to show a sharped syllable, and lowering a finger to show a flatted syllable.

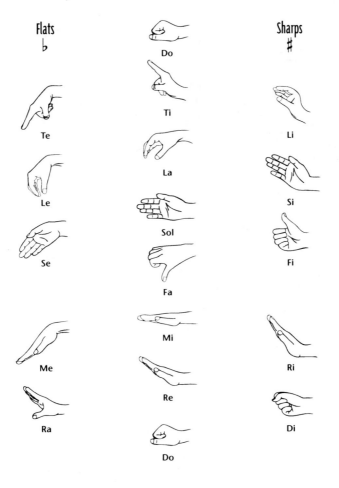

Rhythm syllables assist with rhythmic precision by helping students remember the relationship of sound to time. We are fortunate to have many systems currently in use that can be traced back to the nineteenth-century French Time-Names system.[5] The most common systems in use now are the Gordon, Takadimi, Mchose and Tibbs, and Kodály systems. No matter which system is used, consistency produces accuracy. Refer to *Progressive Sight-Singing*[6] by Carol Krueger for a complete resource of all rhythm syllables.

| SYMBOL | RHYTHM NAME | NOTATION NAME |
|--------|-------------|---------------|
| ♩ | ta | quarter note |
| ♫ | ti-ti | two eighth notes |
| 𝄽 | --- | quarter note rest |
| ♬♬ | tika-tika | four sixteenth notes |
| ♩ (half) | too | half note |
| ♪♬ | ti-tika | eighth note, two sixteenth notes |
| ♬♪ | tika-ti | two sixteenth notes, eighth note |
| ♩. ♪ | tum-ti | dotted quarter note, eighth note |
| ♪♩♪ | syn-co-pa | eighth note, quarter note, eighth note |
| ♪.♬ | tim-ka | dotted eighth note, sixteenth note |

# TUNING FORK

A tuning fork is a tool for musical independence. It is not necessary for a conductor to use a tuning fork to have an excellent ensemble; in fact, many exceptional conductors do not use one. It does, however, require the conductor to use his/her own musicianship to lead rehearsals and models independent musicianship for the singers. Leading rehearsal with a tuning fork can give the teacher more mobility to move around the rehearsal space, and can save time when trying to communicate with an accompanist.

Learning to use a tuning fork can take time. The only way to get faster and more accurate is to practice. A conductor may try to improve skills with a tuning fork by choosing one piece from the programmed repertoire (a piece that is "fork-friendly" for beginners might be in the key of A, D, or another easily-relatable key to the pitch you are hearing). During score study, practice giving pitches from the tuning fork for all parts, at the beginning of each phrase, and any anticipated trouble spots. Sing the pitches, then check yourself with the piano. A piece with fewer voice parts is a good idea to begin with. You may need to have a conversation with your accompanist about your plan to work independently on this particular piece. Letting the choir hear the tuning fork ring on your stand is another way to help train your singers as they begin to gain musical independence.

# PREPARATION FOR EAR TRAINING

There are many excellent resources available for helping you teach music literacy skills to your singers in a progressive sequence. Most sources provide material your singers can use for reading practice. What is often missing in the material is aural preparation for using the material effectively. The following sequence will help prepare the singers' aural and visual readiness.

## Preparation for Pitch

1.  Start with a limited tone set (mi-re-do). Try to connect to a known warm-up or song that clearly features this pattern. For example:

2.  Echo patterns from tone set with hand signs (students sing from hand signs only).

3.  Echo patterns from solfege ladder (students sing from teacher pointing to ladder).

4. Students sing from non-staff melodic contour.

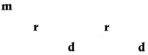

5. Students sing from non-staff horizontal plane.

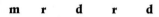

6. Students sing from stick notation.

7. Students sing from staff with no rhythm.

8. Students sing from staff with rhythm.

9. Aurally identify the specific interval or pattern from staff or non-staff notation using fill-in-the blank, multiple choice, hand sign games, etc.

10. Sight-read the specific interval or pattern within a prepared tone set using both stick and staff notation.

11. Repeat this process as you extend the tone set.

## Preparation for Rhythm

1. Select a few patterns. Try to connect to a known warm-up or song that clearly features this pattern.

2. Echo patterns.

3. Use patterns in body percussion.

4. Use flashcards: teacher performs the first two beats on the card, and students perform the last two beats. Expand to students performing all four beats on the card.

5. Combine several flashcards together to make a longer phrase. Then re-order or re-arrange the cards.

6. Aurally identify the specific patterns from staff or non-staff notation using fill-in-the-blank, multiple choice, games, etc.

7. Sight-read the specific patterns.

8. Repeat this process as you incorporate new rhythm patterns.

Note that in Kodály-based general music classrooms, this kind of sequence is built on a repertoire of folk songs that are learned in music class. Having singers come to your choral program from a variety of schools and/or programs, there is not always a common song repertoire for your singers, so using vocal warm-ups can be a good starting point.

# EAR TRAINING EXERCISES

If you use solfege or rhythm syllables in your rehearsal, singers need opportunities to not only become fluent with the syllables, but also to learn how to use those tools musically, with awareness. It is important to note that singing up and down the scale is helpful in gaining fluency, but it will not guarantee that your singers will be able to navigate around the scale or secure intonation with the syllables. Kodály wrote: "Those who try to sing the larger intervals by climbing up the scale will find them but slowly and vaguely. The scale will sound correct only when its 'pillars' are established in advance, and these 'pillars' are the notes of the pentatonic scale."

It is helpful to have students sing pentatonic scale patterns to secure intervals. The teacher will need to model these patterns (vertically) for the students to echo, reminding students that these patterns take time to internalize, and that making mistakes is a great way to learn. Over time, students will build independence and sing these patterns on their own.

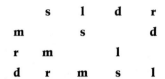

Practice both ascending and descending directions, using a common pitch to start each row. It is not necessary to sing in order from left to right; instead, you may want to experiment with comparing the interval construction of each row.

## Ascending Patterns

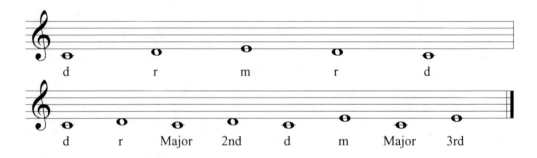

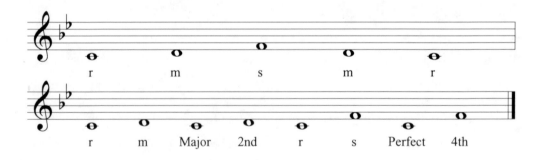

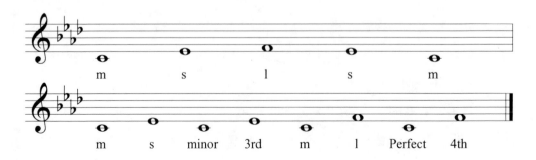

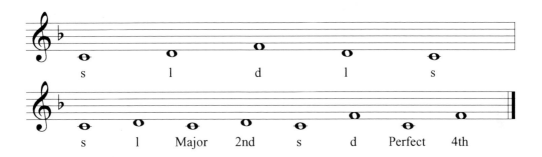

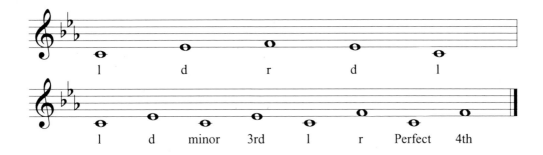

## Descending Patterns

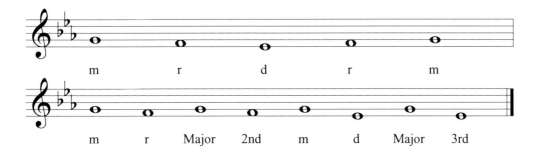

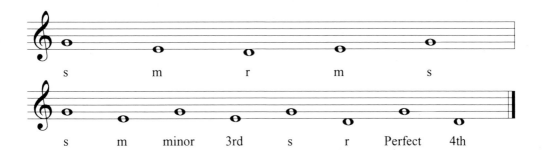

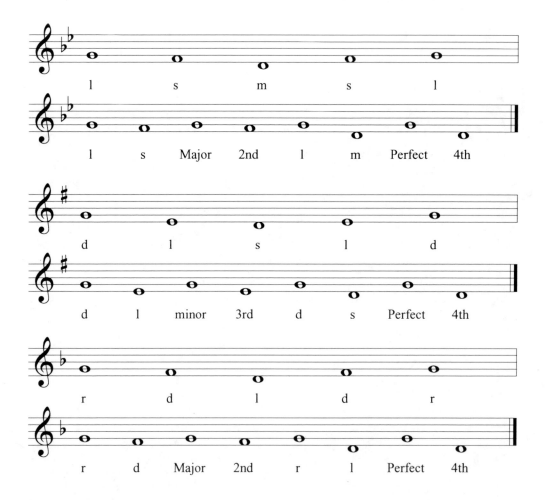

## TWO-PART SINGING

Kodály felt that singing in two parts was the best way to help students develop aural skills: ". . . those who always sing in unison never learn to sing in correct pitch. Unison singing can, paradoxically, be learned only by singing in two parts: the voices adjust and balance each other. Those who have a clear aural conception of the sound C-G [harmonically] will sing the interval C-G correctly [melodically]." Kodály composed numerous musical exercises for pedagogic use, now commonly referred to as the Kodály series. One of his best-known publications is titled "Let Us Sing Correctly,"[8] written specifically to help students improve intonation.

The following exercises can be taught with hand signs or from notation. The main objective is to help students experience the sound of intervals and orient their ears to the ideal acoustic intonation of these intervals when singing a cappella. Echo the patterns with audiation. Sing a pattern with syllables and have students to audiate the pattern in rhythm before prompting them to speak (and then sing) it back.

**Examples from "Let Us Sing Correctly"**

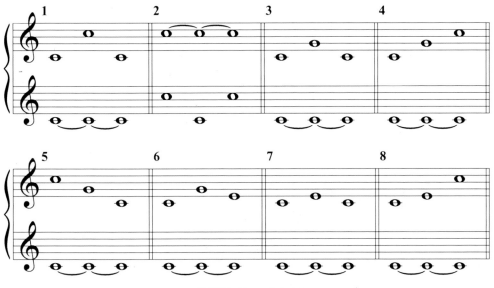

© 1952 by Boosey & Co Ltd.

# DIATONIC INTERVAL TRAINING

The following diatonic exercises strengthen interval relationships, which in turn build the skills needed for instant modulations. Using a common starting pitch requires singers to use their understanding of interval construction. The first pitch can be repeatedly played on the piano as a low drone to ground the singers. First, ask the students to audiate the pattern or use hand signs before they sing. After singers begin to have reliable success, change the order to increase difficulty. Gradually increase the pitch set to the full diatonic scale, starting on every solfege syllable, which results in singing modal scales. The following examples have no specific rhythm. Students can sing on steady pulses or the teacher can create rhythmic patterns for interest, variety, or extra challenge.

### Ascending Patterns

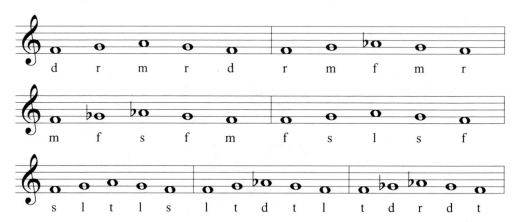

### Descending Patterns

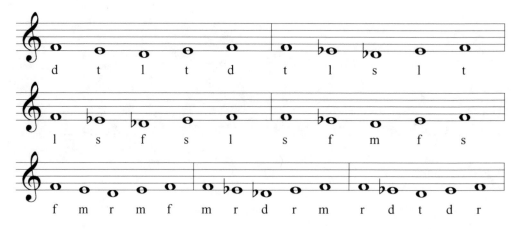

# SIGHT-SINGING

Many excellent resources exist to help singers practice sight-singing skills. The teacher should remember that the exercises are only a portion of the experience, and that aural preparation is the key to success. Of course, singers need to be challenged, but if their aural skills do not match their visual reading skills, they will quickly become frustrated, as will the teacher. Sight-singing is in essence an assessment of the singers' internal aural development.

There are various degrees of difficulty of sight-singing tasks (not referring to the degree of musical difficulty). The eventual desired goal is to give music to singers, allow them to scan it for a few seconds, and then read it. To help singers train to this task, the teacher may want to try a variety of strategies:

- Chant the rhythm.

- Chant the solfege syllables in rhythm.

- Read through silently while the teacher keeps an audible beat.

- Instruct students to chant the downbeat of every measure and audiate the rest.

- Sing the example "out of rhythm" (every pitch equals one beat).

- Teacher sings the first two beats of every measure, students sing the last two beats of every measure.

These are only a few examples of the kinds of activities teachers can use to prepare students for reading longer passages. With practice, students will eventually be able to scan quickly, then sight-sing. It is important to remember that students will excel when they feel comfortable taking risks. Sight-singing is an opportunity to build the safe learning environment as the teacher encourages the singers' effort, bravery, and willingness to take on musical challenges.

# TRANSFER

The most efficient way to work with a choral ensemble in a traditional rehearsal plan is to teach for transfer among the various parts of the rehearsal (warm-ups, sight-singing/ear-training, and repertoire). When rehearsing repertoire, it is beneficial to reinforce vocal techniques taught during warm-ups. When singing warm-ups, it is helpful to reinforce what is being learned during the sight-singing/ear-training portion of your rehearsal.

## Integration of Sight-Singing/Ear-Training During a Warm-Up

Teach a new warm-up with solfege first, then add the text. Or take it one step further and learn a new warm-up using hand signs only, before adding solfege and text. Following a known vocal warm-up, ask singers to decode the warm-up into solfege. Guide the singers as much or as little as necessary to help decode (this activity is a pre-dictation). You may need to help them realize the first pitch is not do. Then sing on solfege. Then sing on text, while "thinking" the solfege.

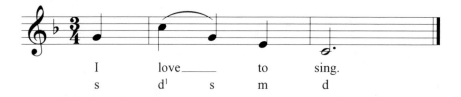

|  |  |  |  |  |
|---|---|---|---|---|
| I | love___ | to | sing. | |
| s | d¹ | s | m | d |

## Integration of Sight-Singing/Ear-Training while Learning Repertoire

Choral ensembles often perform music that is beyond their reading capabilities. Young musicians are quite capable of learning challenging music by relying on their director and/or accompanist. Indeed, they should have the opportunity to perform challenging music as they are developing their musicianship. Incorporating reading skills into rehearsals without compromising the quality of performance is an opportunity for creative teaching and learning.

While teaching performance repertoire, teachers can look for excerpts that can be extracted for isolated study. Following are several examples in which excerpts of performance repertoire are used to improve singers' musicianship skills while learning the repertoire itself.

## "INSCRIPTION OF HOPE" BY Z. RANDALL STROOPE[9]

This activity can be successful with students who have limited solfege and reading experience. It is helpful in activating their ears and making connections between the solfege activities in class and actual notation they sing for performance.

1. Lay out the following four flashcards in any arrangement other than the one shown here:

| d¹ | s | m | s |
|---|---|---|---|
| d¹ | s | m | l |
| f | s | l | s |
| l | t | — | d¹ |

2. Sing a descending scale (in the key of E-flat) and repeat high do again, with instructions to listen carefully to this highest note as it is an important clue.

3. Ask students to listen as you sing the cards (in the above order—which is different than what they see). When finished, they should identify the last card that was sung. Remind them to listen for high do. Move the last card to a new location where the correct order will be assembled.

4. After students correctly identify the last card, ask why they chose it. Answers should relate to high do at the end.

   • Ask students to look at the remaining three cards, while you sing them on a neutral syllable. There are two cards that are very similar, and one card that is quite different. Ask the students to find the places where the remaining cards belong.

   • Once the cards have been arranged in their correct order, ask the students to explain how they were able to hear the difference between the two similar cards.

   • Students sing from the cards using solfege syllables.

   • Using music, show students the melody at measure five and ask them to sing using solfege. You may want to point at the notation to keep track of where their eyes are in the music.

Activities like this can be successful with students who have limited solfege and reading experience. It activates their ears and makes a connection between solfege and the actual notation they sing from in rehearsal and performance.

*for the Nebraska Choral Arts Society and Children's Chorus*

# Inscription of Hope

Two-part Chorus and Piano with optional String Quartet and Oboe*

Z.R.S. and from an inscription on
cellar walls in Cologne, Germany

Z. Randall Stroope
*Quoting a Russian Folk Tune***

## "QUIET SEA" BY JILL FRIEDERSDORF AND MELISSA MALVAR-KEYLOCK[10]

The refrain for "Quiet Sea" has limited rhythmic and melodic material that lends itself well to reading activities. Using rhythm syllables, teachers can lead students through the discovery (or practice) of triplets. The following chart is an example of a flow sequence from known to unknown patterns.

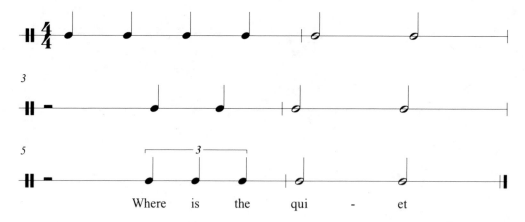

Once the triplet figure is secure, students should practice the rhythm of the refrain. This chart shows the refrain as it is stacked in sets of two measures, which gives a visual cue to how it is organized and how the rhythmic patterns relate to each other.

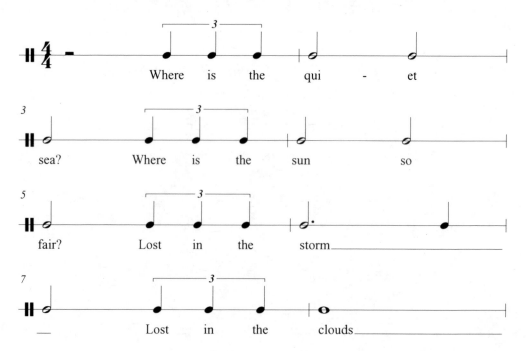

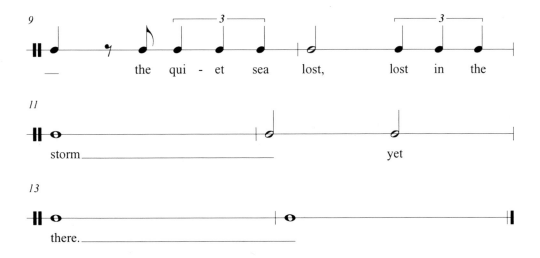

Reading activities can be rhythm alone, pitch alone, or a combination of both. The following pitch exercises can be used to prepare for reading the pitches of the refrain of the piece, or could be used to reinforce pitch reading after the melody has been learned by rote. Teacher can lead singers through the exercises by hand signs, solfege ladder, traditional notation, or any combination of these activities. Exercise #1 corresponds with measures 26–30, exercise #2 prepares singers for measures 33–38, and exercise #3 prepares singers for measures 30–32.

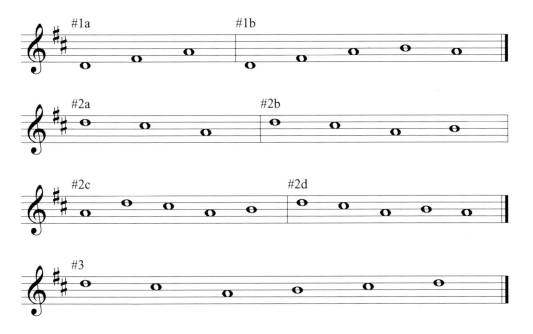

Where is the qui - et sea? Where is the

sun so fair? Lost in the storm

Lost in the clouds_____ the qui - et sea

lost, lost in the storm_____ yet

## CANON BY THOMAS TALLIS

All praise to thee, my God, this night, for

all the bless - ings of the light; keep

me, O keep me, King of kings, be -

neath thine own al - might - y wings.

Pitch and rhythm skills can be taught using performance repertoire, even after the singers have learned the music. The following is an example of a fill-in-the-blank game (pre-dictation) activity. This activity can be done in a variety of ways depending on the level of the choir.

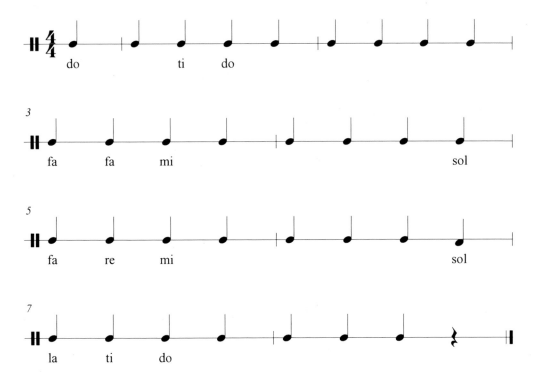

- Display the "fill-in-the-blank" version of "Tallis Canon" shown above. The tone set (answer bank) can be increased or decreased depending on their ability level.

- This activity could be completed on the staff and transposed to additional keys.

- Sing on absolute letter names (A, B, C) from stick or staff notation (also in a variety of keys).

- If the piece is already known, students may use their memory and inner-hearing to fill in the blanks.

- This activity could also be used to introduce the piece, if singers are more advanced and ready for a challenge.

## "KYRIE" FROM *MISSA BREVIS IN D* BY BENJAMIN BRITTEN[11]

The diatonic interval ear-training exercises presented earlier in this chapter can be an excellent preparation for introducing the "Kyrie" of Britten's *Missa Brevis in D*. A whole-tone scale can be used to practice changing solfege syllables to build a pattern (see illustration below). Changing solfege creates instant modulations and requires the singers to listen carefully to the distances between the pitches. This pattern can be changed to reflect the intervals needed in the ascending and descending passages of the piece (whole step–minor third pattern), using the same concept. This process will help singers to have a firm grasp on the intonation needed for the main theme of the "Kyrie."

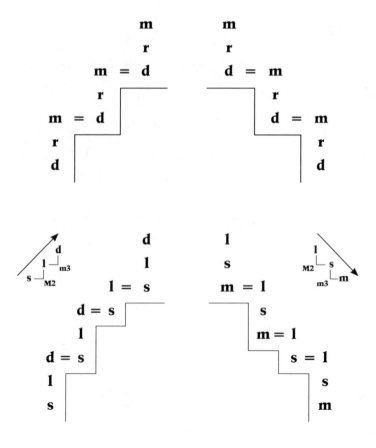

# Missa Brevis in D

for Boys' Voices and Organ

## Choral Score

## KYRIE

BENJAMIN BRITTEN
Op. 63

As shown, teachers can integrate sight-singing, musicianship training, ear-training, and music theory throughout the choral rehearsal. Teaching repertoire in a way that builds musical understanding and musical skill is rewarding for both the teacher and student. Teaching repertoire in a way that provides a stimulating yet safe learning environment builds enthusiasm, musical understanding, and artistry.

*"Real art is one of the most powerful forces in the rise of mankind, and he who renders it accessible to as many people as possible is a benefactor of humanity."*

*–Zoltan Kodály, 1954*

## CHAPTER 6

# COMPREHENSIVE MUSICIANSHIP THROUGH PERFORMANCE

## A STUDENT-CENTERED APPROACH TO TEACHING AND LEARNING

BY KAREN L. BRUNO

As choral educators, we believe that singing in choir is a valuable way to build community with our students. We hope to create a rich learning environment for them in our rehearsals that will challenge and celebrate them as singers. To that end, we search out methodologies that align with our values, several of which are lifted up in this section of the book.

While Comprehensive Musicianship Through Performance (CMP) is included in this section, it is not a perfect fit with the other chapters. Rather than a methodology, it is an approach that cultivates thoughtful, reflective teaching. The methodology (or methodologies) you prefer, the goals or learning targets you set for your students, and the repertoire in your curriculum are all compatible with CMP. If you teach in a school, district, or state that has specific standards you are expected to teach, the CMP template can accommodate them.

In this chapter, you will not find step-by-step instructions, specific resources, or training. What you will find is a brief summary of the flexible planning model that can help integrate and deepen your pedagogy, clarify your thinking, and bridge the music you teach to the lived experiences of your students. But first, one more set of thoughts:

# EDUCATION AND TRAINING

What do you want from your students—curiosity and imagination, or disengaged compliance? What do you want from your professional development—clear answers, or intriguing ideas to contemplate? If we are honest, we probably all want a little of each, for our students and ourselves. I suspect, however, that most of us wish to light a spark in our students and want agency in our own rehearsals. These are values that fall on the imaginative and contemplative ends of the spectra listed above; they are not neatly accomplished in a convenient, step-wise fashion.

While compliance is handy and stepwise techniques efficient, they are aspects of training. Many things in life require training—think of young children who must learn how to brush their teeth, use the toilet, and fold their clothes. We teach them the steps necessary to complete these tasks so they can be habituated and repeated. Teaching can have aspects of training, too—think of the techniques you use to quiet 75 students in a room, demonstrate how to hold an octavo during rehearsal, or show how to stand safely on risers. These are tasks that become routine, that should not require effort to remember or reproduce as time passes.

Education, however, is generally messy. It does not necessarily take place in a linear fashion. It integrates a variety of ideas, builds on them, adds new ones to the mix, and explores others. It analyzes, questions, and speculates. It is important for us to ask our students to use their own thoughts, experiences, and ideas as they learn the music. It is equally important for teacher-conductors to examine the repertoire we choose with a critical eye, to reflect on the choices we make when designing teaching and assessment strategies, and to be responsive to the students in front of us. These are markers of education, not training.

Philosophically, the CMP approach values the education of both students and teachers. Teaching music is something we can get better at if we are willing to be reflective, thoughtful, and honest. Students will be more engaged if their ideas, experiences, and identities are affirmed and included. Using the CMP instructional model allows us to take into account the real people in front of us, and then design music lessons with their needs in mind. It further allows us to take an honest look at our teaching, make informed decisions, and intentionally plan for student success.

# WHAT DOES "COMPREHENSIVE MUSICIANSHIP" MEAN?

As educational reforms rolled through the United States in the mid- to late-twentieth century, general music classes were created to teach specific, quantifiable musical skills and knowledge. In the middle and high schools, performance-based classrooms remained intact, but teachers were expected to include a broader range of knowledge as part of their ensemble teaching. As a result, many symposia, seminars, and curricula were developed as ways to apply "comprehensive musicianship" principles in choral, band, and orchestral classrooms.

In the mid-1970s, the Wisconsin School Music Association, Wisconsin Music Educators Association, and Wisconsin Department of Instruction recognized that many educators were struggling to combine the twin goals of performance excellence and musical understanding. In order to improve music education across the state, these three organizations established a Comprehensive Musicianship Through Performance (CMP) steering committee. This committee identified eight teachers across the state who would document the best practices of their teaching for one year, then collectively create a template for instruction they would use in the following academic year.

At the end of that second year, teachers noted that they felt more energized, that students were highly engaged and had learned far more than the teachers expected, and that their public concerts continued to be of high quality. In short, using their preferred methodology or pedagogy within the newly created teaching template gave the teachers and students a richer classroom experience. This teaching template was adjusted slightly based upon the teachers' feedback, then disseminated to other Wisconsin music teachers at a summer workshop. These workshops have continued annually ever since. Although the workshop takes place on a college campus in the state of Wisconsin, teachers from around the nation participate every summer. A CMP committee of teachers volunteer their time to lead their peers in an exploration of the teaching template and guide participants to write, and later implement, their own teaching plans.

Although forty years have now passed since the original CMP pilot project, the template that uses music selection, analysis, outcomes, strategies, and assessment as points of the teaching model remains the same. One thing that has changed over the years is the exploration and deepening of what is meant by "comprehensive." Rather than simply referring to the need to analyze a score and be aware of a composition's history or the life of the composer, "comprehensive" also refers to the way in which the students experience, explore, and relate to the music-making process, and the way in which a teacher integrates these aspects into a teaching plan for classroom use. The Wisconsin CMP approach uses the term "comprehensive" to describe the integration of theory, history, performance, the musical and nonmusical aspects of students' life experiences, and teacher planning. Including students' lives and teacher planning in this list are factors that set CMP apart from most definitions about comprehensive musicianship, but are arguably the most valuable. The model weaves these pieces together into a cohesive template for intentional music instruction.

# CMP INSTRUCTIONAL MODEL

Committee members have used a variety of metaphors over the years to describe the CMP instructional model. Here are a few:

- The CMP model is a map; the points of the model are the topography. If one knows a place, one knows how it feels, behaves, looks, and sounds. If teachers have studied a piece of music and know their students, they can bring the two together in a way that facilitates deep understanding.

- CMP is a mirror: if you hold the points of the instructional model up to your teaching, it is possible to see the strengths and challenges in your classroom. The model illuminates your teaching values; the choices you make demonstrate your beliefs or expectations.

- The CMP teaching plan is the glissando of choral pedagogy—it is a useful way to stretch our teaching voice, but is not the end goal in itself.

These metaphors are important to keep in mind as you read this section of the chapter. While the CMP model has a template, it is intentionally broad to allow teachers to incorporate the needs of their own students, their preferred pedagogical or methodological systems, and any external expectations such as state or national standards.

The points of the CMP planning model are music selection, analysis, outcomes, strategies, and assessment. A teacher can begin thinking about or implementing the model in any one of these points. The graphic used to depict this is a five-pointed star; each point of the model is connected to the other. Teachers are encouraged to enter into the planning and teaching process at whatever point of the model makes sense at that time. Sometimes, a teacher selects a piece of music first and then mines it for ideas. Other times, a larger instructional goal helps us determine the best piece of music for an ensemble and is, therefore, the starting point. Where a teacher begins in the model is unimportant. What is important *is* that each point of the model works with the others to create an integrated plan.

Music selection, as a title, seems pretty self-explanatory. The goal of this point of the model, however, is to encourage the teacher to articulate what makes the piece musically valuable to include in your curriculum. This is not simply identifying the nuts and bolts of tessitura, difficulty level, and the other practical concerns we always consider. It also means looking for depth, quality, and markers of excellence.

Please note that quality music exists in every genre, including contemporary music. The idea is to carefully choose the very best piece of music possible so that you won't run out of things to explore with your students. While individual taste allows for some subjectivity, it is possible to objectively identify where a piece is on the spectrum of "utilitarian" or "cheesy" to "brilliant." Remember, too, that "simple" can equal "profound." Your high school singers can have a meaningful encounter with a well-crafted canon.

Analysis, of course, goes hand in hand with music selection. How do you know that the piece you choose has markers of excellence? In the CMP teaching plan, "analysis" does not (necessarily) refer to the chordal analysis you did in your collegiate theory classes. Instead, it encourages you to take a deeper look at the music and note the interesting compositional or contextual aspects of it. When you notice these things, wonder or guess as to why they are there. If you notice aspects that can be researched, do it! If there are important cultural underpinnings or performance/teaching practice, learn everything that might be relevant. Look for compositional devices and, instead of just labeling them (motif, sequence, etc.), speculate why the composer or arranger chose to use them. This process will prove useful as you explore the riches of the composition with your students in rehearsal.

Although the term "outcomes" may feel dated, it remains useful to think about what, specifically, we hope to keep in our sights as we design instructional goals for our students. The outcomes in a CMP plan should come directly from the riches you found in the analysis of the repertoire, and they should be transferrable to other pieces. What can this particular piece help you teach well? Why are these goals important for your students? Identifying outcomes will help you prioritize your daily instructional time, as you can plan rehearsals with specific goals in mind instead of merely responding to whatever happens in the moment. Identifying outcomes allows you to decide what, in a piece, creates a valuable teaching and learning opportunity.

Within the outcomes point of the model, teachers are encouraged to identify a skill outcome (what can this piece teach your students to do?), a knowledge outcome (what can this piece help your students to know?), and an affective outcome (what can this piece help your students explore related to feeling, value, opinion, personal awareness, musical mood, etc.?). Thinking through each of these with your students and the music in mind helps us give the students what they need to grow, both musically and personally.

Take, for instance, "Sumer is icumen in," the twelfth century canon. I am beginning to teach vocal independence, so I have selected this slightly more complicated canon. For my skill outcome, I will have students perform music that contains voice crossing while part of a chamber ensemble. My knowledge outcome will be for students to understand the concepts of monophonic and polyphonic textures, and to apply the terms to music they listen to and perform. Since my students live in a cold climate, the affective outcome might be to explore musical companionship across time—how is it possible that a young person, nearly 1,000 years ago, could have been as excited as I am about the return of summer, and used music when celebrating?

Strategies, then, flow from the outcomes you have written. They are the way in which we get our students to explore the goals we identify. Many of us learned teacher-centered approaches: listen from the podium, give feedback to the singers, and then listen for singers to make adjustments and corrections. Thus the rehearsal flowed on.

When writing a CMP plan, teachers are encouraged to consider student-centered strategies, using whatever methodologies you prefer, that give students some agency in the rehearsal. Perhaps this is the opportunity to consider cultural responsiveness in your rehearsals. Perhaps you will design strategies that incorporate your students' musical experiences, preferences, or identities. (For example, the knowledge outcome above could encourage students to bring in music they enjoy listening to and analyze its texture.) Whatever you do, it is important to keep both students and outcomes at the center of your strategy planning. If a strategy is not connected to the outcome you are aiming for, it has become an activity—fun to do, but not purposeful.

In addition, strategies are where we can honestly evaluate whether we are training our students or educating our students. If we want to educate our students, we should design strategies that encourage them to be active, to make choices, to notice, to wonder, to be reflective. Although these types of strategies can be messier, they are richer and, once woven into the regular flow of a rehearsal, do not take extra time. Student-centered strategies keep students engaged, develop trust between student and teacher, and build community in a rehearsal.

Assessment is necessary even when we don't need to assign a grade. In some community children's choir programs, the word "assessment" is absent from conversations until audition time. But assessment is always necessary—it is how a teacher-conductor knows that students have understood the learning target. It gives important feedback regarding how well your chosen strategies have worked, and helps you decide what must come next in a rehearsal.

In a CMP plan, assessment has three steps: gather information about student learning (connected to the outcomes you have identified), evaluate that information by analyzing or interpreting the information you gathered, and then decide how to act upon what you now know—reteach, reinforce, move to a deeper level, etc. Remember to include student-centered assessments at both the formative and summative level to really find out what your students understand, and don't forget to include a variety of learning styles and a range of options for students to show their creativity when designing your assessment tools. If you teach in a school that requires a grade, you can use this data to assign a value as needed. Whether or not you assign a grade, however, assessment is an important part of the teaching and learning process and, when done creatively and well, can give us even more information about our students.

Now, back to the metaphors. As we work through the points of the instructional model, it becomes clear how the CMP process holds up a mirror to our own teaching, why having a map to the landscape of the music and the students is so important, and how the plan itself is simply a tool to practice thinking about how one will teach students, not an end in itself. Others who have encountered the Wisconsin CMP approach have commented that it is "just good teaching." Some who are working with the edTPA for future choral educators note that the CMP model is a similar, but more robust way to plan instruction and use it to help pre-service choral educators have a deeper understanding of the planning process. I hope you can see the flexibility in the model, the way in which it can deepen your teaching, and how it can help you remain student-centered in your rehearsal process.

# WHY STUDENT-CENTERED TEACHING MATTERS

We teach a subject area to which students come with a high level of experience, and with specific preferences. While it is possible that students have not had formal music training at home, it is likely that music has impacted their lives in some way. Music is a part of every culture, and a component of many celebrations or milestones in life. Youth identify with certain types of popular music within their social circles and they create in-groups and out-groups as a result of those affiliations. Music exists in grocery stores, in films and online videos, and in advertising media. To say that a student's first introduction to music is in our choral classroom is flatly mistaken.

In addition, although it seems obvious, we must remember that we teach people, not a subject area. Invariably, one of the reasons you chose to go into this field is to make a difference in the lives of the youth you teach. Giving students choice and input in the rehearsal process gives them the opportunity to notice things for themselves, to share their thoughts and ideas, and to create personal connections to the music they sing. It also shows that you care about and value their uniqueness as individuals.

Note, however, that this does not mean that we should plan to perform only the music students currently care about! Your curricular goals still exist, and the music in which you believe should still be the core of your rehearsal process. Selecting high quality repertoire is still your role, and selecting music just because you think students will enjoy it is not educational. But perhaps students can augment the music you will teach with some of their own in response to your teaching or assessment strategies. Perhaps students can select, from the music you have taught them, which pieces they wish to perform on a concert. Maybe the concert itself can feature their musings, "aha" moments, or other learnings as program notes, short videos, or art projects on display at the performance. This, too, demonstrates to students and parents that the singers are active participants in their education, and that their ideas matter.

Why is this important? In order to build a bridge from our students to the music we teach, we must know where the edge of each shore lies. We can't just know our choral repertoire (although we must!); we must also know our students. When we know our students, we can choose music that will stretch them, select outcomes that help them grow as musicians and as people, and design responsive strategies and assessment tools. If we honor our students as whole people, they are motivated to stay and learn. If we do this successfully, we include those who may feel under-invited to our ensembles, thereby diversifying our choirs so that they represent our school or community.

Once this trust is established, a teacher-conductor can build a community. Engaging singers in the learning process builds on that trust, and creates a safe space where vulnerability—an important component of an art form where one's body and voice (figurative and literal) is the instrument—is accepted and celebrated. Great music that generates rich outcomes designed for your students, taught through student-centered strategies that are frequently assessed for success, almost guarantees deep learning and devoted singers. These factors lead to powerful performances for choir and audience... and extremely satisfied teachers.

# TO LEARN MORE

I have not referenced any part of this chapter, mostly because it would be nearly impossible to do. I have been a member of the Wisconsin CMP committee since 2002, just as Patricia O'Toole was finishing *Shaping Sound Musicians* (GIA, 2003). For a more thorough overview of the Wisconsin CMP project and teaching template, please read her book, which was written with input from the committee.

Since the publication of the book, the committee has continued to adjust how it talks about and teaches the CMP instructional model, both in the summer workshop and in conference presentations or publications. Since we don't yet have a second book in print, I encourage those who wish to engage in current conversations about CMP to attend a summer workshop in Wisconsin. Please visit www.wmea.com/CMP/workshop to find out where the next workshop will be held.

Wisconsin CMP committee members have also advised projects in Iowa and Illinois; each state has developed its own summer workshop. If you live in one of those states, I encourage you to attend a workshop with our colleagues there.

# ACKNOWLEDGEMENTS

This chapter draws heavily from almost fifteen years of meetings, workshops, and conversations between my CMP committee colleagues and myself. I am indebted to their rigorous, creative, and joyful work that inspires me to be the best teacher I can be. Finally, I must thank Dr. Janet Revell Barrett, the Marilyn Pfledere Zimmerman Endowed Scholar in Music Education at the University of Illinois at Urbana-Champaign, who is a friend of the Wisconsin project. In 2016, she attended the summer workshop and provided thoughtful, constructive feedback that culminated in a personal letter to the committee on July 2, 2016. Many of the observations and ideas she brought forth in that letter helped me connect and clarify thoughts that had been swirling in my mind, some of which have found their way to the pages of this chapter.

## CHAPTER 7

# ACCOMPANIST AS COLLABORATOR

BY JAN CORROTHERS

In his book *Collaboration in the Ensemble Arts: Working and Playing Well with Others*,[1] Dr. Tim Sharp defines the term "collaboration" as working together to achieve a goal—a process where two or more people or organizations work together to realize shared goals through knowledge, learning, and building consensus. He defines the "motivation of collaboration" as a common goal held between two or more entities that moves them closer to their mission, that can't be achieved alone, that will not be able to be achieved with current resources, or that will not be able to be achieved as effectively without a partner. These definitions hold true to efforts not only outside of the musical rehearsal, but certainly within them as well. Arguably, the greatest responsibility of a successful choral conductor is to establish and continually nurture the relationship of the conductor-accompanist-choir triangle.

Beyond experience alone, few formal education opportunities exist for pianists to develop the necessary skills and intuition needed to be successful choral accompanists and collaborators. Standard piano performance degree programs, including collaborative piano degree programs, rarely devote an entire course to the art of choral collaboration. A widely accepted myth is that a pianist possessing strong technical skills will automatically be a capable collaborative pianist in a choral setting. This has proven to not always be the case. The terms "pianist" and "accompanist" are not synonyms. A choral accompanist must not only possess strong technical skills, but also a broad range of abilities and intuition that are developed over time and cultivated through experience.

Quite often, choral conductors do not have the luxury of hand selecting their accompanist through an audition process in their school, church, or community program. Instead, they may find themselves in the uncomfortable and perhaps frustrating position of working with a pianist who may be a wonderful solo performer, but does not have an understanding of collaboration within a choral setting. If clear, healthy communication of ideas and expectations from both conductor and accompanist does not occur on a consistent basis, the choir may never achieve its fullest potential.

Many accompanists are successful choral collaborators because they have had the opportunity to sing in a thriving choral program at some point during their education. This experience has enabled them to cultivate their musical instincts by learning how to shape or highlight independent vocal lines within a polyphonic section, to feel the choir's collective breath at a cadence, or to support articulation of melismatic sections requiring a diaphragmatic "bounce," for example. These elements may not come naturally to a pianist who has never sung in a choral ensemble.

The relationship between conductor and accompanist must be regarded as a team. The most critical element of a successfully functioning conductor-accompanist-choir triangle is respect. All sides of this triangle should have mutual respect for one another as musicians, identifying and promoting one another's strengths. The singers must be aware of and regularly observe this mutual respect between its leaders. This supports a unified team and strengthens the morale of the ensemble, which ultimately enhances its overall musicianship and performance.

In January 2013, a survey by this author was given to various respected choral conductors and accompanists across the country, in which the responses were presented during a Chorus America interest session at the University of Cincinnati - Conservatory-College of Music. The conductors polled were encouraged to share insight and perspective on the following questions:

- What qualities do you need, or hope for, in a capable choral accompanist when you serve as a guest conductor/clinician in a festival or honor choir setting?

- What qualities do you desire in a capable choral accompanist with whom you collaborate on a consistent basis (church, community, or academic ensemble)?

- Is there a difference between the two experiences (one- or two-day vs. long-term collaborations)?

18 of 30 conductors polled addressed the qualities that they desired from a capable choral accompanist when serving as a guest conductor on a short-term basis: shows confidence in their skill set and musicianship, supports the conductor's artistic vision, breathes with the ensemble, anticipates the conductor's needs in rehearsal, takes pleasure in the creative and collaborative process, serves as an extra set of ears, gives honest feedback if asked, is a team player, is able to lead a sectional if needed, gives starting pitches without being asked, has a positive attitude, can play open score at tempo, has a neutral facial expression that doesn't display judgment, has a pleasant expression that demonstrates enjoyment of the process, gives attention to nuance as initiated by the conductor, is able to play warm-ups, commits to the tempo established by the conductor, is flexible enough to put aside preconceptions in cases where the conductor brings a differing point of view, is assertive but cooperative, is an equal leader, is fun to work with, intuitive, and possesses a high technical skill level, strong rhythmic integrity, artistic sensitivity, keen sense of ensemble, and awareness of dynamics.

While most conductors stated that their answers to question two were the same as question one, additional qualities for consistent collaboration included: totally dependable, attentive, offers feedback between rehearsals, possesses a consistent team spirit, always maintains professional integrity, has the ability to learn another's pedagogical approach, shares in the teaching philosophy, intuitively moves in sync, is friendly to the singers, establishes a relationship/friendship with the singers, is always reliable, displays pride in the performance product, has a love of people, is loyal to the organization, is punctual, focused, and prepared, is open to feedback, and is a good personality match with the conductor.

Noted differences between short-term and long-term collaboration from question three were that while both try to achieve the same end and purpose, the pacing is different. These conductors showed a tendency to have more patience with accompanists in short-term collaborations than in long-standing relationships. In long-term scenarios, they advocated that accompanists get to know the singers by name and establish a friendship, as well as cultivate the intuitive relationship between conductor and accompanist. The building of a partnership and relationship of trust is more probable over the long-term.

The same survey questions were posed to 15 experienced accompanists across the country to generate informative insight as to their preferences in collaborating with capable choral conductors. 12 responders shared the following qualities as desirable when collaborating in a festival or honor choir setting: clearly communicates (both verbally and with gestures), is willing to share the musical or interpretive vision, is willing to discuss roadblocks in the score ahead of time when possible, uses words of invitation and suggestion rather than command and demand, displays public and private respect for the accompanist, offers grace for mistakes when the accompanist is sight-reading, displays open communication during rehearsal, refers to measure numbers rather than just a word or phrase in the score (particularly if the text is not in English), uses the rehearsal time effectively for optimum results, establishes good rapport with the singers and actively engages them, is passionate about the music-making process, doesn't over conduct the accompanist, possesses a sense of humor, extends kindness, acknowledges that the accompanist is a trained musician as well, has an inspiring personality, chooses challenging, edifying, and exciting music appropriate for the age group, is complimentary of small successes, avoids correcting the accompanist in front of the ensemble, is courteous and willing to listen to suggestions offered, and shares the rehearsal plan with the accompanist prior to rehearsal.

For long-term collaboration, the accompanists surveyed reinforced their answers from the first question, but added that when appropriate, they desired that conductors use accompanists as a sounding board and/or advisor with the choral ensemble, both because they will know the group as the conductor does and because such collaboration will foster a sense of investment and ownership that will help maintain quality work. The ongoing working relationship with the accompanist must not be taken advantage of by ignoring or forgetting their contributions. Music being provided to the accompanist well in advance of rehearsal is always appreciated and often necessary. Accompaniment is typically intended to speak as strongly as the sung pitches and should be recognized as such.

The accompanists surveyed stated that the primary difference between short- and long-term collaboration is relational. Ideally, the long-term relationship with an ongoing accompanist goes beyond the rehearsal or performance and is one that needs to continually be nourished and appreciated. A capable choral accompanist will come to know the conductor's strengths and weaknesses and be able to support them in both, enhancing the conductor's strengths. In some cases, this may occur to some degree even in short-term alliances. However, it can truly be magnified with ongoing work that results in great presentations because both are able to intimately know one another on a musical and interpretive scale and truly care about one another. All aspects of the music-creating experience can be enhanced and solidified when the conductor-accompanist team works well together both in and outside of rehearsal.

In the festival setting, the guest conductor must quickly teach and "sell" the music, getting the best quality possible, all while realizing the experience is not going to be perfect—it is to be an inspirational mountaintop experience. With the luxury of time that the guest conductor does not have, the long-term conductor creates a *community* while the choir works toward their goals. This building of community allows each individual to feel he or she is vital to the music making process, and that by working together, more can be achieved than ever imagined.

Personal insights from the experience and perspective of this author in regard to short-term collaboration suggest that the first few moments of the first rehearsal with a newly formed ensemble will determine how successful the final performance will be. In the first moments, both the conductor and accompanist discover the capabilities and limitations of the other and establish their "playing field." They determine what they have to work with and begin making adjustments, if needed, to create their ultimate musical product.

The qualities of a capable choral conductor in the festival setting, from the viewpoint of this author, include: being supremely prepared (knowing the score inside and out), being musically intelligent (able to coach and interpret varying styles accurately), consistently acknowledging their level of respect for the singers and collaborators, challenging and pushing the ensemble while offering praise for small achievements, and possessing a personality that encourages enthusiasm and a willingness to sing. When a conductor clearly inspires the team, both the ensemble and the collaborators will sing and play accordingly. This helps foster a healthy, functioning triangle.

The accompanist should seek to acquire respect from a guest conductor upon first meeting. Once that is established, the leadership team is formed. Respect puts all parties at ease so that together, they can work to teach and inspire what will become *their* singers. The choir will recognize this very quickly. If singers sense tension between the conductor and accompanist, they will not sing as effectively as a cohesive unit. Once the triangle of conductor-accompanist-choir is in sync, moving in the same direction with mutual respect, inspired learning and true artistry can occur.

From this author's perspective, it is beneficial for conductors to invite accompanists to play with appropriate touch, articulation, and phrase shape, always supporting the desired tone from the ensemble which promotes good listening even during choral warm ups. When reading through a new piece, if helpful, the accompanist should play the melody line with enough of the left hand, or bass line, to help provide a tonal center, particularly if the melody is disjunct. If the melody is played by itself, it leaves singers dependent only on the notes they hear from the piano, rather than allowing their ear to help recognize and grasp the harmonic progression. When more than a single line melody is introduced upon first read through, incorporating too much accompaniment too soon may lead to incorrect note learning and ultimately confuse the singers. During an interlude or section of the introduction or ending that is marked "free" or with rubato, it may be appropriate to allow the accompanist to appropriately interpret that section without being conducted.

No matter how advanced the level of a choral accompanist, it is imperative that they have their pencil ready to make markings in their score that the conductor instructs the singers to write in. If the conductor is creating a mental image for the singers to help them communicate or express a particular phrase, the accompanist should also insert that idea at the same place within their score. That imagery will transfer to their emotions, as well as their ultimate support of the ensemble through their playing. The singers will not only feel it as they sing, but they will sing into the way the accompanist expresses and supports them, resulting in a unified musical experience that is most gratifying to the listener and performer. Again, this requires equal participation from all sides of the conductor-accompanist-choir triangle.

In an ideal relationship of trust, when appropriate, a conductor may ask what the accompanist is imagining as they play, or what source of inspiration supports the way they express their part on the page. It is optimal that all sides of the triangle are inspired by one another to strengthen the bond of creativity. Being an integral part of creating artistry from the piano bench is a privilege. The culmination of clear communication, a cultivated skill set, a relationship built upon trust and respect, and passion for the music-making process as a team can be extremely rewarding and deeply satisfying. The rehearsal space and performance stage have the possibility of becoming a safe haven for all contributing musicians, allowing them the freedom and spontaneity to be a part of something larger than themselves. When all sides of the conductor-accompanist-choir triangle function at their healthiest, a connection with one other, as well as the listener, happens naturally and true artistry is created.

# PREPARING THE PERFORMANCE

# TOUCHING THE HEART WITH ARTISTRY

BY ROBYN LANA

What are the elements of artistry? Included in such a list is beautiful tone, being musically expressive, refined ensemble and blend, and integrity to the score. Intonation is also essential. And of course, engaging the singers' facial expressions will certainly add to the performance. Yet, the root of artistry is often the last thing conductors bring into the rehearsal process. Deeply and sincerely connecting to the music is a key to artistry that must be incorporated throughout the learning process.

## LAYING THE FOUNDATION

Laying the foundation for artistry will set a standard for the immediate rehearsal, as well as for the year to come. Begin by strategically seating the ensemble. With youth, it is very helpful to seat complimentary voices together. Anyone who has sung in a choir knows the challenge of singing next to a voice that clashes with their own and causes muscular tension as they sing. When empowered by a voice that compliments, singers can sing confidently and make adjustments in their color and technique based on what the conductor presents from the podium. Simply seating by height, even for a performance, is not the optimum environment for the ensemble. When placing the singers, I like to have the color I am aiming to create in the section seated in the back. I will put the voices with the most depth in the middle, and the lightest voices in the front. I find this mix of colors balances the section, while bringing unity throughout.

Creating a seating chart based on complimentary voices can be time consuming, especially if the ensemble is large. My ensembles at the Cincinnati Children's Choir and Xavier University both begin their season with this exercise. A new piece is introduced, often in simple unison, but occasionally in two or three parts. In just a few minutes, it is taught and then a magical game of "memory" begins—auditory memory. One at a time, each singer performs a few measures. Just like the card game, new voices are "flipped over" so the room can hear them. The entire room listens for like sounds. When a voice that is similar to another is identified, we have them sing together to see if there is a match. If so, they are moved next to each together and removed from "play." As others match their color, they will be added to the same row. Once seated as a section, the entire section will sing the same passage. The combined sound demonstrates evidence of the successful process, which often serves to calm the nerves of those whose turn is still to come (singing alone in front of their peers). Instead, they are part of the "game" and enjoy the challenge presented to their ears. With an ensemble of 85 or more, this can take the better part of an entire rehearsal, but it sets the standard and expectation for the entire year and is worth the investment.

Likewise, setting the standard for each rehearsal begins during the warm-up process. Technically, the human voice does not require a muscular "warm-up" as an athlete does. But engaging the voice in unified technique for the ensemble (many sing for other conductors and each choir has its own sound based on the teaching of its leader) and mentally fusing the choir so that they are physically and cerebrally involved sets the standard for each rehearsal.

## CONDUCTORS ARE EDUCATORS: TEACHING THROUGH THE MUSIC

When introducing new repertoire, conductors must always be educators first. It is a joy to observe conductors of the most advanced ensembles who still engage their choirs in the educational process. They use imagery to present their ideas, offer suggestions for unifying the sound and blend, prompt their singers to sing through the line, discuss how various voice parts interact and engage each other, and teach about the style and historical significance of each work. The techniques of these fine choral conductors work well with trained, professional musicians, but they would be equally effective with children and young singers, simply adapted for the readiness level of the singers being taught—not "dumbed-down," but broken into more elemental segments.

Always teach *through* the music. Empower the singers to hear, analyze, and evaluate themselves, so they are mentally engaged. For example, find the tonal center. Sing a moveable do scale, using Curwen hand signs, in the key of the octavo. If the piece is tonal, sing phrases and voice parts on solfege. If the piece has passages that are dense with chromaticism or tone clusters, knowing where each voice part sits with solfege will allow the singers to find anchors to which they can return. For example, in Lee Kesselman's "The Friendly Beasts,"[1] the final verse has many points where parts are a step away from each other. Without a foundation in solfege, maintaining such harmonic tension would be extremely challenging for any singer, especially an inexperienced one. However, such a piece presents an opportunity for rich harmonic success for the choir, when a proper solfege foundation is first established. When sight-singing becomes a part of every rehearsal, part of every score study, the choristers will become independent musicians with skills that will transfer to future choral experiences.

# CONNECTING THE CHOIR TO ARTISTRY

Every child, every person, has a different style of learning. As educators, it is our responsibility to discover how to successfully teach each singer in our ensemble. Research has shown that learning styles involve different parts of the brain. Some styles relate to certain individuals more strongly, but engaging many learning styles will engage more of the brain, as follows:

- Kinesthetic: Movement involves the cerebellum and the motor cortex (toward the back of the frontal lobe).

- Auditory: Aural learning involves the temporal lobes.

- Visual: Using diagrams and visual aids involves the occipital lobes (back of the brain).

- Social: Doing group activities (such as identifying solfege in a score with a small group) involves the frontal and temporal lobes.

- Individual: Working alone (such as individually writing in solfege in preparation for rehearsal) involves the frontal lobe.

In a choral rehearsal, kinesthetic learning can come from self-conducting, drawing the line of a phrase with one's hands, or swaying as an ice-skater in triple meter. Allowing the choir to move to the music can solidify the tempo during a challenging passage, just as the members of an orchestra move and feel the music they are playing through their bodies. Auditory learning usually takes place through demonstration. It is helpful when the conductor can provide a vocal model. If that is not possible, identify a singer who can, use a recording of a choir that can be a strong model, or bring in outside singers who can model and help guide. This is often most helpful when a woman is working with boys' changing voices, or a male teach would like a vocal model for his young girls. Auditory learning can also involve imagery. Help the singers draw a mental picture of the story of the text they are singing, then find a way to bring that story into their reality by relating it to a movie or television show with which they are familiar.

Visual learning can be a simple as pointing out the color of a shirt and asking the choir to sing that color. They will change their tone with each bright yellow, royal blue, or grey. Put stretchy bands in their hands to help them visualize tension and release kinesthetically. Visualize a cut-off or particular entrance through a conducting gesture and interpret the difference in what they see. This is closely related to social learning, the main part of a choral rehearsal, in which students are regularly listening to and interacting with each other, leading to an understanding of how their voice part relates to the others around them.

Individual learning will be experienced when there is preparation on the part of each chorister, whether learning and recording their part so a teacher can hear individual progress or writing markings in the score. For example, sing through a specific phrase with the choir and then ask them to decide how to indicate the phrasing through slurs and breath marks in the score, based on what you, the conductor, have just demonstrated.

# INDIVIDUAL EXPRESSION

As discussed in Chapter One, creating an environment in which all are safe to create and explore is essential to singing artistically. The voice is the most personal instrument and is reliant on a healthy body—mentally and physically. Creating a safe environment will also open students up to the risk of individual expression. Explore the poetry of your repertoire early in the rehearsal process. Understand the historical significance, the poet's intentions, and any possible hidden meanings of the text. Analyze the text with the chorus, and discuss the text painting that occurs in their voice parts or the accompaniment. This could be as simple as a flowing piano part to indicate moving water or tone clusters to indicate tension in the text. In Kesselman's "The Friendly Beasts,"[1] each verse paints a picture of the animals of the manger: donkey, doves, and sheep. A deep understanding of *why* the composer has set the music in a particular way will allow the music to come to life off the page.

Facial expression must also be a part of the teaching. A choir communicates with listeners through their voices and their bodies. Facial expression cannot be successfully added at the final hour of rehearsing, just before a performance. Rather, it must be an automatic element of how the choir expresses each piece. Just as someone may say, "I love to travel," but uses a monotone voice and no facial expression, the listener will assume sarcasm and that the speaker actually prefers to be in the comfort of their home. But when the eyes brighten and there is inflection in the voice, the listener not only believes the statement, but also will likely be curious about where the speaker has traveled during their life! The same is true for a choir. A choir can perform with precision, perfect intonation, and advanced ensemble skills, but will that be enough to touch the hearts of the audience? Will that be enough to make the listener want more?

# ADDITIONAL RESPONSIBILITIES OF THE CONDUCTOR

What the choir sees is what they will sing. A high conducting gesture will not allow for a full, deep breath. A floppy wrist and arm that is unclear where the beat is will not keep the ensemble united in tempo and phrasing. The gesture matters! Especially when the conductor teaches the ensemble to sing what they see. Responding to the gesture enables for less talking in rehearsal and more productive communication between conductor and chorister. When the conductor trusts the ensemble to respond, the conductor will be able to adjust tempi, dynamics, entrances, cut-offs, and all aspects of the performance based on the energy and strength of the ensemble that day or the needs of the performance space that may differ dramatically from the rehearsal space. When possible, record the concert. At the very least, audio record it. Listen to what went well, as well as to those moments that were not completely what you had intended. Learn from them. What impacted the singers' sound? Was it what the choir received from the conductor? Were the singers connected and engaged?

The more musical knowledge and independence the choir has, the less the conductor needs to micro-manage the music. Some styles require the conductor to simply get out of the way. Allow the choir to enjoy the moment and be a unifying force while enabling them to shine and operate as an ensemble using their ears, eyes, and mental connection to each other to guide the performance. Very importantly, as a conductor, never trust your inner ear. Listen with discernment. Teach the choir to self-evaluate. Assess and discuss performances and their impressions. It is worth the rehearsal time, as it demonstrates respect for the performance experience and student opinions, while enabling the ensemble to move, together, to a higher level in the future.

## CHAPTER 9

# PROGRAMMING
## PUTTING TOGETHER A CONCERT

BY ANTHONY TRECEK-KING

The art of putting together a program is one that often gets left to the last minute. Giving thought to the order of the selections is part of the process, but it takes time to construct a concert that both leaves an impression on the audience and is enjoyable to perform. The art of organizing the many elements that make up a concert is one that should constantly be nurtured. With a few guiding philosophies, you will immerse the audience in a journey that will, in some small way, create a lasting impact beyond the individual selections.

Before a note is ever rehearsed, the path to engaging concerts begins. The good news? There are many "right" answers when it comes to programming. It's just a matter of finding the one that works best for you, your singers, and the audience. As Kenneth Phillips states in *Directing the Choral Music Program*,[1] "It is important for the audience to understand the choral director's job as educator and not entertainer. Each concert is really a recital or presentation of what has been learned in the class." Conductors are all essentially educators.

Setting and meeting educational goals through the programming process should be a major part of the design. This is particularly important for youth choir directors who are always thinking about the development of both the individual singers and the group at large. These goals can be broken down into specific elements like style, vocal development, theatrical understanding, and performance skills, as well as educating and entertaining the audience. The excitement comes when all of these threads converge into intense artistic expression.

# CONCERT LENGTH

It is rare that a choral concert lasts over two hours. Concert venues and audience members are both interested in finding creative, less time consuming ways to engage with arts organizations. When considering the length of a concert, keep in mind two important factors: the endurance of your singers and the endurance of the audience. Long concerts, particularly with young choirs, can tax the singers to the point of both mental and vocal fatigue. Likewise the audience has only so much tolerance and a program that is too long may not be well received. Unless you have programmed an extended work, plan on a concert length of between one and one-and-a-half hours. One of the finest compliments you can receive is a plea for more.

Children and youth choir organizations often present multiple ensembles on a single program. How many pieces each choir will perform should be considered well in advance. When it comes to tallying up the total time allotment, remember to include stage transitions, any speaking or announcements, and applause. Remember, if combined with the music selections, the total is more than two hours, cuts should seriously be considered.

What about intermissions? Concerts over an hour-and-a-half in length should allow for an intermission; however, keep in mind that an intermission presents an opportunity for audience members to leave. This is especially tempting for parents, family members, and friends of singers who have finished performing before intermission. One way to address this problem is to make sure that all singers have a part to perform on both halves of the concert. That being said, keeping the audience and singers absorbed through engaging programming is the goal, not simply figuring out a way to hold the audience captive. Working with young children can be extremely rewarding and witnessing them perform on stage can be trilling. Singers of a young age (or really any age, for that matter) have a point where they will "expire" and no longer be able to stay focused. This "expiration point" can be triggered by length of time, time of day (more on this later), or some combination of both. If your program runs past this point, you will be dealing with a whole different set of problems.

Gaining in popularity is the mini- or even micro-concert. This is a concert of 45 minutes or less, focused in some way to create a cohesive performance. This will limit your repertoire choices and that number of ensembles that may be included on the program; however; it is a very attractive option for children and families to attend, as well as an easy entry-point for first-time audience members. You may also find it easier to construct, in some ways. While putting together a shorter concert may feel like it is constraining the artistic expression, it forces the conductor to distill the concert theme and objectives down to their very essence. Think of it like a TED talk—sure, most presenters can give an hour-long lecture, but do they have the ability to deliver a high impact, informative demonstration in less than ten minutes? It is always better to leave your audience wanting more than to have them check their watches.

# PROGRAMMING PHILOSOPHY

Creating interesting programs for children and youth choirs gets complicated when considering the educational goals of the arts organization. As an educator first, the director must consider the singers' development when constructing a program. Therefore, music selection is one of the most critical roles an educator can fulfill. From the music flows the curriculum. With that in mind, let us consider a few different philosophies for constructing a concert program: topical, thematic, and smorgasbord. Each has its own appeal. Often, multiple approaches will be used to create a complete concert season, as can be seen in the programming choices of most major choral organizations. One of the best things a young conductor can do is to get his or her hands on as many different concert programs as possible. Looking at what pieces or composers are being programmed and considering how they are organized is an invaluable way of generating ideas.

## Topical Programming

One of the easiest ways to organize your selections is to arrange them according to common attributes. Period, country, and culture are examples of broad topics one can use to organize a concert. This approach is attractive due to its generous ability to include a wide range of selections. With topical programming, there is usually not an attempt to construct a narrative, but the pieces all have a common link that binds them together. Let's consider a December holiday program. These programs are often constructed using a topical approach. The music selected is connected to the holiday season, but there may not be a further narrative within the concert structure. This allows for music from many cultures to be included, as there are different holiday celebrations that occur during the month of December.

## Thematic Programming

A thematic program can be defined as any concert program that pertains to a specific theme. This theme not only connects the music, but also attempts to construct a larger narrative. So, what is the difference between thematic and topical programming? Topical does not attempt to tell a story, but seeks to include pieces surrounding a central idea, whereas thematic programming seeks to deliver a message beyond the pieces themselves. While both are useful ways of putting together a concert, thematic programming goes a step further and attempts to create a deeper experience for the audience.

When putting together a thematic program, one should clearly define the narrative itself and consider how the order of the pieces may aid in conveying the narrative to the audience. Having a well-defined narrative is not only helpful for the audience, but for students in rehearsal as well. The singers have a thirst for information about the music they are singing, and if they know what the concert program is trying to accomplish, then they will better be able to express that idea to the audience. In addition, the rehearsal journey will be more enjoyable. Programming with a theme in mind helps to unify the music selection and compels the director to explore literature with which they may not be familiar. The narrative does not have to be explicit to have the desired affect. Take the season of autumn. While you could collect a number of selections that all relate to this time of year, why not explore the many interpretations of the word "autumn" found in literature and music, such as a time for giving thanks, a time to reflect, a time to rest, or even the end of life.

Should one select a topic or a theme first, and then find the music to fill that program, or work from the music to find the theme? Finding quality music that fits your educational and developmental objectives should come first; the concert theme will often follow. (This is a departure from programming for adult organizations with purely performance objectives. Youth choir conductors should be concerned with the educational growth of the individuals in the choir first.) Cast a wide net and collect more scores than you may need. Once you have a strong core of selections, look specifically for pieces that can be connected together. Themes often evolve through this process, ending somewhere beyond where you began. Remember that thematic programming with strong educational and social goals are best constructed over time. Rushing this process often yields unsatisfactory results.

This being said, sometimes educational and musical objectives can only be met by setting a theme first and then programming towards that theme. The theme itself becomes the educational goal and the music selections then serve that theme. The Boston Children's Chorus annual Dr. Martin Luther King, Jr. celebration is an example of the theme being the educational goal.

## Smorgasbord Programming

Anyone who has ever worked with young singers (especially within a large organization where concerts include multiple choirs at various skill levels) understands that a tight theme can be too restrictive and may actually create a barrier to successful programming. In this instance the smorgasbord approach is a possible solution. Try to use a broad title to which all conductors and choirs can contribute. A title like "Spring Concert" may be generic and cliché, but it is helpfully simple and may work for your situation. Catchall titles, such as "Music from A to Z" or "Around the World in 80 Minutes," are broad. Most likely, the repertoire of each individual ensemble will have selections that fit. When using the smorgasbord approach, the order of the pieces is just as important as with the topical and thematic approaches. But you will need to dig into each selection's musical characteristics to find a satisfying sequence.

# MUSIC ORDER

After you have come up with the theme and selected all of the music, it is time to put them into a specific order. Unlike an orchestral concert where you have just three or four works, the choral director often will have ten or more selections. The concert order becomes almost as important as the individual pieces themselves. The director should consider tonality, style, language, instrumentation, mood, voicing, and staging when putting it all together. Much like selecting paint colors for a room, the concert program can be complementary, analogous (monochromatic), or contrasting. The goal is to create an order that seem inevitable.

It may be useful to consider a few different options and then wait until you begin rehearsing the music until making a final decision. Regardless, the first pass at the order should be considered temporary until a few weeks before the concert. This will give the conductor and the singers a chance to live with the repertoire to see if all of the pieces will be adequately prepared. Do not be afraid to make changes to the program if you find that particular piece that is just not working. Having a great experience should be the goal, not simply getting through all of the music.

One question that baffles many conductors is how to begin and end a concert? The prevailing thought is that you open with a piece that is loud and energetic, and end the concert with something that is light and up-tempo, such as a folk song. While these are excellent ways to begin and end a concert, it is also predictable. Why not do the unexpected? It can be very effective to begin the concert with a piece that draws the audience in. Select a work that has an uncluttered texture and a medium slow tempo. The director may choose to begin the concert without music and rather opt for a dramatic reading that connects the spoken word to the theme of the concert. There are so many possibilities! A surprisingly effective way to end the concert is with a piece that is thoughtful and concludes gently. For example, sing an arrangement of "Amazing Grace" followed by the choir humming the melody in unison while recessing from the stage. The audience is left in silence only with their thoughts.

Chronological ordering is the easiest method to apply to a given set of music. Here you start with the earliest time period and move chronologically through the selections ending with the most contemporary work. This is one of the go-to standards when programming and often conductors stop here without looking deeper into the selections. Examination of the pieces' individual characteristics often yields a more satisfying result. Also consider how you may be able to group your selections by language, culture, composer, text, texture, or historical time period. For example, group two pieces from different composers that set the same text. These larger groups can then be ordered themselves, working towards the final program order. Lastly, you can connect the pieces in a group together and perform them without applause. This can be particularly effective at the beginning of a concert.

Nothing kills a concert faster than having too many of the same pieces in sequence. This is especially true when the pieces share multiple characteristics. For example, if they are all written by the same composer, start in the same key, have similar textures, and progress at roughly the same general tempo, someone in the room (singer or audience) will become bored. Instead, why not intersperse them with contrasting selections? It can be particularly effective to use an unexpected juxtaposition that shocks the listener. This can be exactly what the audience and your singers need and, if used with purpose, can even deliver a strong statement.

Consider your singers and your audience as you create your order. Following a work that is lengthy with another long work may fatigue everyone. With young voices, physical stamina is important. Juxtaposing multiple pieces that reach the outer limits of their tessitura can be fatiguing. Consider the harmonic progression of the program, which can be ordered in a way to create interest and motion throughout the concert. In addition, varying the texture and instrumentation throughout the program can be very powerful. The order of music has an effect on the listener. Therefore, it is important to be deliberate with that effect.

The space between each piece is an opportunity to add interest. Try to keep the concert moving without having to stop for set changes. Stage transitions (adjusting the standing position, adding/subtracting instrumentalists, changing choirs, etc.) are often not thought through and become "dead air" during the program. Instead, this time can be incorporated into the programmatic scheme by adding a reading or even a musical transition. Carefully planning the stage transitions will greatly improve the overall experience for the audience and choir members. Smooth and effective stage transitions can dramatically cut down on concert times. Spend time in the performance space beforehand, thinking through how the transitions will be accomplished. Remember to build time to practice them into your final rehearsals.

## STAGING

One unique experience is watching a great orchestra fill the room with the performers kinetic energy. It is infectious and enhances the overall experience. Choral musicians should take note and think about what natural kinesthetic motion are present while singing. How can the face, arms, and body be employed to accentuate the selections? This is not necessarily choreography, but rather using the placement of singers and their natural movements to accentuate the text. After all, when we communicate with each other, even on the phone, we are physically active. The first step is to encouraging singers to engage physically during rehearsals and performances. Remember, singing is an athletic event. Working with a stage director or an acting coach can greatly enhance the singers' abilities to perform on stage.

Providing alternatives to the "park-and-bark" choir on risers can heighten the concert experience. Every performance space is unique, supplying a creative opportunity to place the singers. Time spent thinking about how best to work within each space is well spent. Simply adjusting the standing formation on the risers can have surprising visual impact. Try spreading the singers outward or compacting them inward from how they would normally stand. Extend forward towards the audience, leaving fewer singers on the risers. Even forming geometric shapes while on stage can be a welcome change. Once you begin to think about how visual staging can add to the overall experience, the possibilities are endless.

The accompanying photograph shows Calderwood Hall (located at the Isabella Stewart Gardner Museum in Boston, Massachusetts), a square performance space that is on four levels. Each level above the floor is only one row deep. If seated on the fourth level (third balcony), all that is typically seen is the tops of the singers' heads. This photograph shows several singers performing a piece while lying down, giving the audience in the balcony a unique experience. Breaking the barrier between the performer and the audience is another way to enhance the performance through staging. The easiest way to accomplish this is through a processional/recessional or a call-and-response. Immersing the audience in sound by surrounding them with singers can also be quite powerful.

Another element not often considered in the overall scheme of concert construction is lighting. A lighting plan, even a simple one, can greatly enhance the experience. Don't know anything about lighting? No worries! Find a lighting director to help you construct and execute a plan. If you do nothing else with respect to staging, adding lighting might be the biggest bang for the buck. The advantage that a chorus has with respect to staging is the ease of setup. Generally speaking, singers only need themselves, giving conductors the flexibility to create a visually appealing performance. The possibilities are endless.

# CONCLUSION

To bow or not to bow, that is the question. Much has been written on whether or not a choir should bow at the end of a section or the concert. Some even have very strong opinions and well reasoned arguments either for or against bowing. If there is not going to be a bow, then the choir members should stand and look pleasant smiling at the audience. They should not fuss with their music, fix their hair, or (worst of all) look bored and/or talk to one another. Remember, the audience is clapping in appreciation for the work of the group. If bowing is the preference, then it should be practiced to the point of looking clean.

Putting all of the various pieces together to form a compelling concert order is no easy task, but it is a task that is well worth the effort. The ideas and thoughts expressed in this chapter are just a few examples of how a conductor may construct a concert from its various elements. If you think back to a concert that deeply impacted you, or one that took you on a journey from the first note well past the last, consider how that concert and its elements were thought through very carefully. The music selection matched the singers with respect to both educational and musical goals. The order of the music was planned according to a topic or theme. And finally, the choir was staged in combination with lighting to be visually impactful. When all of these elements align, something special almost always follows.

# GENDER-SPECIFIC TEACHING

## CHAPTER 10

# OH BROTHER! SUCCESS WITH BOY SINGERS

## (BOY OH BOY—BROTHERS SING ON)

BY JULIAN ACKERLEY

The exquisite beauty of the treble boy singing voice is beyond compare. Boy singers have played a significant role in western civilization music for centuries. But being a boy in today's world can be challenging. Emotions are often shut down in a macho mentality. Boys are generally energetic and curious, yet also very sensitive to how they are viewed by others, especially their peers. They have split personalities. Boys can be loud, boisterous, vulgar, rude, crude, and insensitive to others . . . and at the same time, they can be polite, emotional, helpful, responsible, and excited to learn. When a boy shows up to your rehearsal, you never really know which boy he is that day.

Emotional literacy is an important aspect of male development. Boys need to be helped in cultivating their emotional awareness, giving them the vital connections and support they need to navigate the social pressures of youth. Music can help them through their development; however, the lack of males in vocal programs has been a problem for many years. There has been significant discussion on the reasons why this is so. As music educators, we all strive for fresh new approaches to motivate students and keep music programs vibrant. Who would like to have more boys and men in their choirs? For most choir directors, the likely answer to that central question is a resounding, "I would!"

# THE PSYCHOLOGY OF BOYS

There is extensive research and literature available about the fundamental psychology of boys. Four books* of particular insight include:

- *Raising Cain* by Dan Kindlon and Michael Thompson
- *Boys Should Be Boys* by Meg Meeker
- *The Wonder of Boys* by Michael Gurian
- *How High Should Boys Sing* by Martin Ashley

The collective research and perceptiveness of these authors can support those dealing with boys in any situation, including music instruction and choirs.

Social forces threaten boys by teaching them to believe that "cool" equals manly strength and stoicism. Boys often receive detrimental emotional training, sometimes from those closest to them, such as their fathers, older brothers, and other male friends. Boys can experience major mood swings as they struggle to find their identities.

The way boys feel about themselves has an effect on how they live. Self-esteem is an opinion, not a fact, and a person's outlook can be transformed. Boys' ideas about themselves are molded by experiences in the family, at school, at church, in sports, from friendships, and in wider society. Human nature is to seek approval. Yet our culture does not easily give encouragement. Intolerance and chauvinism is universal. If a boy is musical, artistic, hardworking, or smart, he is often liable for mocking from peers. Thus, in dealing with boys, especially in re-direction, it is important to be affirmative and constructive while being sensitive to their feelings without embarrassing them.

Extensive brain research discovers how a boy thinks and how that is different from girls. Boys are a composite of their biology and influences of their environment. Testosterone plays an undisputed part of male development, as does their surroundings and interactions with others in evolving attitudes and emotions. In boyhood, rules and boundaries are key and boys can feel lost without them. In most instances, boys like structure. They don't think they want to be confined by regulations, but there is a comfort for them in understanding limits and knowing what to expect.

* A complete list is included in APPENDIX A.

# ARTS AND ATHLETICS IN A BOY'S LIFE

Boys like sports. They like to run and play. But it is not necessary for sports and music to be at odds in a boy's life. A well-rounded child generally has opportunities in the three As: academics, athletics, and the arts. Other elements significant in the balanced maturity of a young man are family, spiritual development, and community service.

Some parents label their sons by making statements similar to, "He is our athlete," or, "He doesn't do many sports. He is our artistic one." These messages are unhelpful to young men who are learning behavior and attitudes from their models, primarily their parents. Arts and athletics do not need to be exclusive of each other. Boys certainly can have experiences in both. Clearly, commitment and priorities become factors when a boy and his family consider his youthful pursuits.

Some aspects for success can be found in both choir and organized sports, including teamwork, focus, self and group discipline, camaraderie, and enjoyment. Here are a few other similarities:

- Sports have practice sessions to prepare for the game.
  Choirs have rehearsals to prepare for the concert.

- Sports have their matches in front of a crowd of fans.
  Concerts are performed in front of audiences.

- Winning the game can produce exhilaration.
  A successful concert also evokes intrinsic emotion.

Coaches have asserted that games are won at practice. In choir, the primary music education happens in the regular rehearsal and not necessarily at the concert. Even though there is an instructive value in performing for an audience, basic music literacy is developed during consistent rehearsals. This represents the significance of the process (team practice or choir rehearsal), which is ultimately showcased as the product (the game or concert).

One difference between sports and the performing arts is the competition aspect of the contest. Athletes have a game plan that is performed in a precise period of time. There is a set of established rules. But much of the time, the participants act in response to their opponents. They deal with the constant element of surprise and must develop skills in reacting to the other team. There is spontaneity and uncertainty that leads to excitement. The outcome of the competition is not known, often not until the very end of the game. Choir concerts are different. There is the same intense preparation but, hopefully, the performance is more predictable, without the constant element of surprise. Of course, that is not to say that some concerts don't have unexpected moments, but there isn't the same need to react to someone else's action.

The benefits of participating in both sports and the performing arts include mastery of skills, valuing preparation, goal setting, attitude regulation, leadership opportunities, collaboration, time management, friendship, a comprehensible sense of order, and self-control. Choral conductors working with boys have the opportunity to minimize stereotypes and allow young men to flourish in multiple endeavors, allowing the arts to coexist with athletics in the building of a better boy.

# THE BOY'S CHANGING VOICE

It's no mystery that boys' participation in choral music is greatly reduced during the middle school years, which is when most boys experience the voice change process. Historically, the topic has been researched by the likes of Duncan McKenzie, Irving Cooper, Frederick Swanson, and John Cooksey with various methods of voice classification.

*Choral Journal,* the American Choral Directors Association publication, has many articles on the voice change and was the forum for a dialogue between Henry Leck and Patrick Freer on the subject. Henry Leck, of Butler University and the Indianapolis Children's Choir, began the debate with his May 2009 article, "The Boy's ~~Changing~~ Expanding Voice."[1] The article was a follow-up to his video *The Boy's Changing Voice.*[2] Leck supports high voice singing during boy voice change. The byline on the video and article is "Take The High Road." He advocates working down from head to chest voice, developing head tone as low as possible.

Patrick Freer, music education professor at Georgia State, rebutted in his February 2010 *Choral Journal* article, "Foundation of the Boy's Expanding Voice: A Response to Henry Leck."[3] Freer's rebuttal includes a reference of the work of McKenzie, Cooper, Swanson, and Cooksey. He supports making a distinction from boys singing in general as opposed to boys singing in a choral ensemble, upon the notion that singing should be taught to all students.

Choral conductors can use a mix of both high and low voice. In essence, there are three vocal classifications: true treble, emerging voice, and changed voice. As Leck has observed, some boys are hesitant to sing in their high voice in social settings. They are afraid of embarrassment; their personal esteem is at risk. Some boys are also reluctant to sing in high voice for a female instructor. If that is the case, find a male singer to work with your boys as a vocal model. Some boys just don't feel like men when they sing high. As we have previously reviewed, this attitude is a sociological problem that must be overcome in a larger scale setting.

Some of the realities of male voice change include boys' need to negotiate erratic shifts, vocal strain, in-audibility on certain notes, breath control issues, and unpleasant tone quality. Boys should be reminded that natural singing is merely extended speech, regardless of what stage of vocal transformation they may be encountering. Boys don't stop talking during voice change, and there is no reason for them to stop singing.

Music teachers should be equipped with answers for boys in voice change. Know the instrument and the anatomy of change, and share what is happening with them. Prior to puberty, a boy's larynx is small and his vocal cords are thin, resulting in a voice that is higher than an adult's. But as he goes through puberty, the larynx gets bigger and the vocal cords grow significantly longer and thicker. His voice gets deeper and the pitch of the sound he produces becomes lower. The slower vibrations of the thicker vocal cords result in lower pitches.

In addition, the facial bones begin to grow. Cavities in the sinuses, the nose, and the back of the throat grow bigger, creating more space in the face in which to give the voice more room to resonate. As a boy's body adjusts to this changing equipment, his voice may "crack." This process lasts a short time. Once the larynx is finished growing, the boy's voice won't make those unpredictable sounds.

Voice change is different for each boy. Dealing with a group of changed, changing, and unchained voices can be challenging. Use "sirens" to explore all areas of the vocal range of both the old and new voice. Have them sing descending scales from high to low moving through the passagio. On the way down, tell them to raise their hand when they think they have started singing in their new voice. It is an insightful experiment and fosters awareness of their voice change and vocal ability.

Allow boys to decide to take vocal rest if needed. But tell them you cannot know that they are resting during a rehearsal. They must stay sitting up and looking engaged. Otherwise, they will always choose to be in vocal rest, sitting back and dealing with their "vocal fatigue." That won't work. Let them find their comfortable range and allow them the opportunity to sing when they can and lay out when they can't. They can leave out certain notes and still be successful. Give them ownership of their individual vocal care. Conductors should be open regarding voice change. Talk to the boys about it. And talk to the girls for that matter. The worst thing to do is to ignore it and let the boys fend for themselves. That's when they head for the door.

# REPERTOIRE SELECTION AND ADAPTATION FOR BOYS

In many ways, repertoire selection is the hardest part of the job. The choral conductor needs to find music of high artistic quality, in a variety of genres, accessible to the singers, and with an appropriate text for boys.

In your search, rely on the research of others. There are recommended literature lists from professional associations such as Chorus America, American Choral Directors Association, and the National Association for Music Education. Reading sessions are another good resource. If you can't attend one in person, contact your local music dealer to request a packet for review. Share libraries with other choirs, churches, and schools. Borrow, but don't forget to return. Attend concerts—you may get many ideas, not just music. Review publisher catalogs. Be careful, as you always want quality repertoire in every style.

Write your own arrangements. To accommodate boys' changing voice:

- Transpose pieces up or down

- Swap parts, such as the tenor and alto, to stay in range

- Have the boys sing an octave lower when necessary

- Double parts

- Write a new part altogether

Use the Choral Public Domain Library and other websites on the internet. Many websites offer a sample of the print music, as well as a sound clip recording. Work for variety. Be sure to include serious music at all levels from the youngest to the most experienced singers.

# BOY RECRUITMENT AND RETENTION

In our current time, boys do not always engage in singing opportunities. It is not uncommon for young choirs to be mostly girls with few boys. Boys have the same innate musical abilities as girls, but often do not choose participation in choirs. Conductors are faced with a recruitment and retention issue for boy singers. This has been an ongoing dilemma.

What goes on in the rehearsal room is ultimately a recruitment tool. The conductor must provide an atmosphere that is inviting, interesting, challenging, and fun. It is also essential to find ways to ease peer pressure. Here are several suggestions to help boy recruitment:

- When possible, advocate for boys to have their own chorus. If that's not possible, at least let them have their own group within the larger mixed ensemble. Boys are much better in many ways when they are by themselves. This peer support will help them if they encounter harassment. Vocal issues can be dealt with in a safe environment that minimizes embarrassment, especially in front of girls.

- Find boy-friendly music. Start the group with an upbeat piece that will grab their attention, so that the fun starts right away. As time goes on, introduce other styles. Boys love beautiful, slow music as well as upbeat, fun selections. You just need to have a plan of when to use what repertoire to maintain interest and cooperation. Help create and sustain an overall positive attitude through the careful programming of quality literature.

- Establish a "bring a buddy" program where boys already in choir are invited to bring their friends.

- Keep boys singing through their voice change by giving them the proper tools to use their head voice.

- Participate in boys honor choir programs, allowing your boys to be around other boys who like to sing.

- Make opportunities for boy singers to interact with older male singers, to let them see the admiration and approval bestowed on guy singers.

- Community outreach is helpful for signing-up boys. Depending on your situation (school, church, or community choir) there are different parts of the public to which you may want to reach out. You might use publications (fliers, newsletters, posters, and press releases), the internet (information on your own website, email blasts, social media such as Facebook, Twitter, YouTube, Pinterest, and Instagram), or broadcast media (radio, television, and cable networks).

- Program a musical or, if you are unable to accomplish a full-blown production, perform scenes from a musical. Boys usually enjoy elements of theater, such as storyline, costuming, sets, and props. It is simply structured play and boys love to play.

- Communicate to parents the value of their son's participation in choral music. There are many activities available to young people. You must convince the boy and his parents of the value of being in choir.

Once you have boys recruited, keep the choral program demanding, fast paced, and enjoyable. To retain boys, create an *esprit de corps* in which they learn to work together, set goals, and have fun. Teach solid vocal techniques that will give them confidence. Affirm their musicianship and their maleness. Pump their egos. Oh, and be sure to have fun!

# GROUP MANAGEMENT FOR BOYS

The only true discipline is self-discipline. In reality, a conductor cannot make singers do anything. Others cannot impose behavior, at least not effectively. How a person acts and reacts is a choice. Generally, children function well with routine and order. Music educators need to create an intrinsic desire in singers for self-control. It is important to train them to make good behavior choices because they want to do so, not because you imposed those choices upon them. Make it their choice. Let them know that it is up to them to be the best they can be.

Keep it positive. Attitude is everything. It is amazing how important a part attitude plays in the pursuit of excellence. Bad attitudes are destructive and often times contagious. There is a place for sternness in redirecting, but it is very important to have judicial use of raising your voice. Avoid power struggles, especially in front of other students. Nobody ever wins.

When a situation requires a reprimand, do a quick redirect. Call out the boy's name in the process, which gets his attention and ensures that there is no doubt about who is being redirected. Do not let the admonishment interfere with the flow of the session. Use humor to your advantage; after all, aren't we having fun? If the infraction necessitates a private conversation with the offender, be sure it doesn't become personal. Tell the boy he is a good person, but he is making bad decisions.

For a major discipline problem that requires parental involvement, consider telling the boy that it is up to him to tell his parents about the problem and to have them call you. This makes him accountable for his actions. You will know if he has followed by whether you get the call from his parents.

"We can all sing at once and create beauty, but when we talk at once we create chaos." There are multiple methods to effectively get the group's attention. Shouting really doesn't work. Students just talk louder over the shouting. Plus, shouting is negative and our goal is to keep things positive. A few methods that work: singing a pitch for the students to match, mouth percussion such as, "tch-tch-tch-tch-tch," and clapping a rhythmic pattern that the singers repeat. Pacing is everything, particularly for boys who can be easily distracted. Keep them busy. In your lesson planning, be sure to have a balance of intense and relaxed periods.

*Excellence is an attainable goal.* Sometimes we expect too little of children. Set the bar high for choristers and let them know that they are capable of doing just about anything. Students will only achieve what you expect from them.

# VOCAL PEDAGOGY FOR BOYS

Methods for teaching boys about healthy singing are not significantly different from methods for other singers. However, the boy voice is a distinctive and temporary instrument that reaches its beauty and agility prior to the voice change process. The purity of sound has been admired for centuries.

When training boys, the fundamental concepts of vocal production are the same as for all singers. Working for a vibrant, open tone quality is rudimentary. This is achieved through unifying vowels and enhancing the blend throughout the ensemble. Young singers respond favorably with imagery such as singing with a round sound, a tall vowel, or vertical vowel. Other aspects of musical singing include proper breath support, phrasing that is natural and uniform, and exploration of a full dynamic spectrum for expressive and sensitive singing. Precise diction, clear consonants, and articulated releases are also central.

*The most important part of singing is listening.* Singing in tune is the product of listening. Blend and a pleasant choral sound are achieved through listening. Two listening techniques that work well with boys are rehearsal buddies and huddles. When intonation and pitch matching is problematic, instruct singers to pair off and face each other (larger groups can simple face each other in a circle). Have them listen to their buddy as they sing. These huddles are particularly helpful when introducing parts. When everyone in a section faces and listens to each other, the part is learned much faster. Huddles also work well for blending.

Practice does not make perfect. This is contrary to the saying of which musicians are very familiar. Reinforce the importance of practicing *correctly*. Practicing with bad technique is not beneficial and generates bad habits. However, practicing properly can help you achieve perfection.

# MAGIC OF MOVEMENT

Boys are constantly on the move; their kinetic energy is omnipresent. Music educators might as well organize the movement. Don't expect boys to sit still for an entire rehearsal. Find ways to get them up and moving whether it is stretching during warm-ups, clapping rhythm patterns, or getting into their huddles. Movement will keep them engaged.

Incorporating movement also applies to the performance. Unless an audience member has a visual impairment, choral music is a visual as well as an aural art form. *People listen with their eyes.* Stage presence is an important component to the choral performance. The audience watches while they listen. Be sure that the boy singer understands that a pleasant stage persona is part of the overall package. Work with them to lessen the fidget factor and frowning. If the performers look like they are enjoying themselves, it will be conveyed to the audience.

When your singers first walk on the stage, train them to look at the audience with a big smile on their face. It is remarkable how that one thing sets an upbeat ambience for the rest of the concert. Also, program the first piece to be something the choir knows well. This minimizes any anxiety and sets the standard of musical quality from the very start. *You never get a second chance to make a first impression.*

Though boys are generally on the move, their coordination is not always the best. But simple movement can enhance the performance. The uniformity of everyone doing the same movement at the same time can be impressive. If you plan to use choreography with boys, here are some suggestions:

- Be sure they know that they are first and foremost a choir. Movement should not detract from singing.

- Simple movement is often the most effective. Don't over choreograph.

- Crisp, clean moves look the best from a distance.

- Exaggerate everything, as it is all just an illusion.

# THE DEVELOPMENT OF GENTLEMEN

Working with boys in a choir is much more than singing choral music. Equally vital to the task is the development of "gentlemen" through concentrated character growth. You can help your boy choristers attain essential core values including responsibility, sincerity, integrity, reliability, and honor while being nurtured in an encouraging environment.

Always take advantage of opportunities to empower boys to be respectful. And they need self-respect before than can respect others. Many challenges face educators in dealing will rude and ill-mannered boys. But the goal should always be to set a standard where graciousness and courtesy are insisted and celebrated. Your expectations of boys being polite must be consistently communicated to them and praised when achieved. Otherwise the impolite behavior will just continue.

In essence, you can incorporate an etiquette program for your singers. It actually is not as daunting a task as initially perceived. Once set in place and maintained, boys will thrive and discipline issues will be significantly decreased. Good manners are always a worthy skill for youth to develop.

Leadership training and service to others are other characteristics of cultivating gentlemen. *Everyone has a choice in life, to be a leader or a follower.* Boys should be encouraged to lead by example and not by words. Working with the group is far more effective than barking orders at them. Train singers to be flexible and problem solvers with a "can do" viewpoint to minimize barriers to their success. Assign various jobs to boys to build individual leadership. They will feel good about their contribution and acquire the important skills of management and teamwork. The significance of helping young men develop character and moral values cannot be overemphasized. We build a better tomorrow by building a better boy today.

## MANAGEABLE—HIDDEN TREASURE—GENTLENESS—STRENGTH

Plato, the classical Greek philosopher, observed, "Of all the animals, the boy is most unmanageable." The energy of boys is remarkable. If you observe a group on any given day, you are liable to see boisterous youngsters running, poking, playing games, and generally having fun. Activities where jumping, sprinting, darting, dashing, and yelling are involved are natural in their existence. As previously noted, boys love to play.

Harnessing that vigor can be a challenge. Choral conductors working with boys have an exceptional opportunity and responsibility to channel boys' energy into a positive experience. Singing in a choir offers a structured environment where self and group disciplines are necessary for success. With clear expectations of what is and what is not appropriate, as well as consistent utilization of redirecting when necessary, the unmanageable become manageable. Each boy learns his individual significance to the team effort while still having fun.

American author and humorist Mark Twain is credited with, "There comes a time in every rightly constructed boy's life when he has a raging desire to go somewhere and dig for hidden treasure." Curiosity is another significant aspect of being a boy. Inquisitiveness seems inherent. Boys love to ask questions, or better yet, discover answers on their own.

Choir offers many opportunities for discovery. Through the study and performance of choral music, choristers learn the skills of basic music literacy. This process can be creative when learning is captivated in fun. For instance, children enjoy playing the "sol, la, mi" game. The object is to recognize pitch through solfege syllables. They think they are competing in a game, but in actuality they are learning the concept of pitch as well as increasing auditory skills so important to singing.

Many community-based boy and children choirs, as well as school and church choirs, provide travel opportunities. Singers who tour are given additional chances for focus on their curiosity. Traveling and performing when young is an experience unmatched. The people met, cultures exchanged, and places seen provide a global perspective that will stay with them through their entire life. National and international travel is certainly an occasion to go somewhere and dig for hidden treasure.

Finally, the early seventeenth century French bishop of Geneva who later became a Roman Catholic saint, Francis De Sales, is quoted, "Nothing is so strong as gentleness; nothing so gentle as real strength." Choral programs offer social skills development to boys. Responsibility, reliability, commitment, leadership, initiative, and interest in the arts are all traits nurtured in choir. Singing boys develop into "gentle-men" while building strength in integrity and character.

Working with and motivating boys can be complex, but enormously rewarding. Choral conductors have the privilege of recruiting and engaging boy singers, helping them to manage their behaviors, discover hidden treasures, and develop gentleness and real strength.

## CHAPTER 11

# GIRL CHOIRS
## WHERE GIRLS FIND THEIR VOICES

BY KAREN L. BRUNO

For hundreds of years, boys have sung in boy choirs in churches, royal courts, and music schools. The Vienna Boychoir, one of the first examples of a modern-day community choir for boys, was formed in the early 1920s, but is a direct descendent of the Viennese court boy choirs founded in the Middle Ages. With the exception of choirs formed in convents or orphanages, there were no similar choral opportunities for girls until very recently. Until January of 2014, not a single girl choir had sung in Canterbury Cathedral—a church that has featured boys' voices for more than 1,000 years.

The number of community-based boy choirs and children's choirs rose in earnest after World War II, but there is no definitive point at which girl choirs began to increase in number. Historically, women's choirs existed in convents, colleges, and small social circles, but none of these were the direct precursor to the community girl choir organizations that exist today. What role, then, do community girl choirs play in the landscape of choral singing? How do they differ from children's choirs? Is it important to separate girls from boys in public school choirs? Is this legal, post-Title IX?

It is difficult to write a chapter about the importance of girl choirs without feeling fraught with potential pitfalls. Rather than resorting to stereotypes or anecdotal evidence, this chapter will include references to research completed in recent decades. It begins, however, with the assumption that the reader agrees with the following assertions:

- Choral singing is an active process. To be successful, a singer must be fully engaged in the rehearsal.

- Since the voice emanates from the body, singing is a deeply personal experience. There is no instrument to hide behind, or to "blame" for a malfunction, and a singer will likely feel as if she is being asked to "take risks" within a rehearsal setting as she learns new things.

- The learning process involves trying something new, failing (to a degree), assessing failure and success, and then trying again, using the assessments as a guide. Learning can be both hard work and joyful.

- Choral music is a vehicle to something "more than" the notes, rhythms, and texts. While choral teachers want to have exciting aesthetic experiences with their singers, they also know that there is real, life-changing power in the process of creating music together.

In recent years, researchers have completed many studies of girls' success in the classroom and women's success in the workplace. These studies cite aversion to risk-taking, negative body image (often driven by media portrayals), and lack of confidence as specific barriers to success for women and girls. While building capacity in these areas will not magically fix the gender gap that exists in many schools, industries, or organizations, doing so will certainly empower girls to more successfully combat the challenges they face as they grow. Since most choral organizations include leadership, social justice concerns, or other personal growth objectives in their mission statements, why not tailor this list to the documented needs of girls? Girl choirs can focus on music as a vehicle to develop the confidence and competence necessary to develop self-assured, successful women.

## ACHIEVEMENT, COMPETENCE, CONFIDENCE

In 1992, the American Association of University Women Educational Foundation completed a study that found a clear gender gap in public school education. Some reasons for this achievement gap were that girls received less attention from classroom teachers,[1] that curricula marginalized or ignored the contributions of girls and women,[2] and that curricula for young children perpetuated gender stereotypes.[3] Subsequent studies show that girls have made gains in some academic areas but still lag in measures of confidence.[4] The AAUW developed a list of recommendations for teachers, administrators, and teacher training programs to address this achievement gap and its causes, but it has not done a follow-up study to document where or how these recommendations have been implemented, nor what specific progress girls have made.

It is clear, however, that there have been very few teachers trained to avoid gender bias in the classroom or the curriculum; there is little time in today's teacher in-service trainings to discuss strategies that promote equity. Rather, time is often devoted to introducing materials and technologies that support the nearly ubiquitous Common Core standards. Time will tell whether or not these new materials include the changes recommended by the AAUW in regard to issues of power and gender more than 20 years ago.

While it is both convenient and easy to blame teachers for giving less attention to girls in a classroom, journalists Katty Kay and Claire Shipman point out how girls are socialized to "be good." They write, ". . . many girls learn to avoid taking risks and making mistakes. This is to their detriment: many psychologists now believe that risk-taking, failure, and perseverance are essential to confidence building."[5] In a classroom dominated by boys who are comfortable shouting out answers to questions, or in a mixed choral classroom where the teacher has been taught to ". . . be sensitive to the needs and interests of upper elementary and adolescent students, especially males,"[6] it is difficult for girls to feel as if they are allowed to be heard, both literally and metaphorically. Indeed, the positive reinforcement received by girls in mixed classrooms when they are being passive rule-followers ". . . discourages them from experimenting with the more active, risk-taking learning styles that would serve them better in the long run."[7]

Obviously, teachers of girl choirs do not struggle with giving less attention to girls than to boys; girls in girl choirs must engage in the rehearsal process or there will be no music making. Sustained engagement can be a new skill for young women who have habituated passivity. In regular classrooms, and often in the world around them, girls are encouraged to express certain feelings but not others like independence, competence, or control.[8] Combining this assertion with the statement that ". . . success correlates as closely with confidence as it does with competence",[9] it is clear that a girl choir teacher's job is to help singers acquire competence through the engaged learning process in order to instill confidence. Competence in the arts takes many forms: not only does a chorister learn to be accurate in regard to pitch, rhythm, and text, she also learns collaboration, persistence, and how to sustain focused attention as she sings in an ensemble.[10] While learning to "be accurate" may seem to directly cause the finding that ". . . women feel confident only when they are perfect,"[11] in fact, the learning process is about trial, error, receiving feedback, and making decisions based on a variety of acceptable options. In the arts, students learn that there is a range of "right" answers—the only "right" answer for any given performance is the way in which that particular ensemble has chosen to perform it. "Perfect" does not exist in the arts world, although it is possible to achieve at a very high level.

In a study of data collected from the National Educational Longitudinal Survey about arts and performance, researcher James Catterall completed a follow-up survey with public school arts participants who had aged into their twenties. He found consistent connections between those who had strong arts experiences in their younger years and overall success as adults.[12] His research also suggested that developing competency in the arts is particularly important for students who otherwise might feel isolated or excluded.[13]

"Confidence," Kay and Shipman write, "is the stuff that turns . . . thoughts into judgments about what we are capable of, which transforms judgments into action. Confidence accumulates through hard work, success, and failure. The natural result of low confidence is inaction. When women don't act, or hesitate because we are unsure, we hold ourselves back. If we channel our . . . hard work, we can make our brains more confidence-prone. What neuroscientists call plasticity, we call hope."[14] Although this quotation refers to women, it is important to teach confidence to girls before they become women. If confidence accumulates through hard work, then it goes hand-in-hand with competence. At the end of a rehearsal process, we present a performance. Girls demonstrate their competence in public and receive positive feedback for their artistry. They take the skills they have learned and reapply them starting with the very next rehearsal. They have gained confidence through authentic means, not through empty platitudes or external rewards. The choral rehearsal process is an important and effective way to build confidence and competence for girls, and thus is a precursor to their future success.

# REPERTOIRE

The AAUW study indicates that curricular materials for girls are often devoid of positive role models or messages.[15] As choral music is our curricular material, a girl choir teacher should keep these specific needs in mind when selecting repertoire. Whether that means singing music written by women, studying texts by women, performing music about women, singing a song in first-person whose text is gender-neutral, or singing songs that break stereotypes about what a girl or woman can experience or be, a girl choir singer may see new possibilities in herself and in her future. Many women's choirs have thoughtfully considered this issue, and composers such as Joan Szymko have provided a wonderful array of empowering and inclusive music for women's choirs. Often, however, women's choir music isn't a perfect fit for girl choirs due to range, complexity, or text. Therefore, girl choir teachers must think more broadly.

Consider the desire to program a piece that has a slower tempo, allows us to teach long lines and phrasing, and is in compound meter: should we program a lullaby (there are many to choose from), or something that evokes imagination, wonder, and action, such as Eric Thiman's "Path to the Moon?" While there is nothing inherently wrong with a lullaby, we can be fairly certain that the role of "mother" is one that our girl choir singer will have been exposed to elsewhere. If we are looking to program music by a woman composer, why not look to Emma Lou Diemer's "Bee! I'm Expecting You!" or Alice Parker's "Escape at Bedtime"? Both have well-known texts that are expertly set, are not terribly difficult to sing (but are through-composed and vocally independent from the accompaniment), and have gender-neutral characters. Diemer scores "extra points" because the poem is by Emily Dickenson, but Parker wins if we want to give girls a first-person narrative that is adventurous and involves breaking rules (another form of risk-taking).

Repertoire is particularly important when it comes to middle school girl choir singers, for textual and artistic reasons as well as vocal needs. Too many compositions for middle school singers are musically trite and contain texts that are, frankly, vapid. Middle school girls crave depth, creativity, and aesthetic experiences; they don't always want to sing about love, or about friendship, or an arrangement of a popular tune that doesn't really work in a choral setting. Girls experience a range of emotions as well. Allow them to explore the variety of emotions that make us human, make "ugly" sounds, or sing texts that our grandmothers might consider "un-ladylike." Let them sing the grisly text of "Ladybird" by Zoltán Kodály and learn about historical events that led to 150 years of division in Hungary. Have them sing the Stephen Hatfield rendition of "Tjak!" and discuss whether or not it is culturally appropriate for a girl choir to perform. Give them "Aglepta" by Arne Mellnäs and let them make scary sounds as they evoke a curse against an enemy. Find a song whose text illustrates what it was like to be female in earlier times, what it's like for women or girls in another culture, or study the opportunities available to a woman composer. Then, compare and contrast to the opportunities, depictions, or restrictions they are faced with in today's world. Exploring a topic together that allows girls to exhibit authentic feelings allows them to integrate anger and caring,[16] which creates both confidence and community through solidarity.

Selecting repertoire with intention allows us to push back against the stereotypes that surround us in the media (why not encourage boy choirs to sing a lullaby in order to counteract movies like *Daddy Day Care*?), which helps us expand the ways in which all youth see their future. Girl choir texts need not read like a feminist manifesto, but they should expand the ways girls see themselves in the world.

## MIDDLE SCHOOL CHALLENGES

Although the term "middle school" is wide-ranging (some districts define middle school as young as fifth grade, others as young as seventh; most end in eighth grade with a few also encompassing ninth grade), we can safely refer to this time period in a child's life as the years during which she will go through puberty. Unfortunately, too many conversations in regard to teaching middle school choirs focus on recruitment of boys (ignore the girls—they will show up anyway), retention of boys (make sure *they* love the music—the girls will sing anything), and teaching of boys (get the boys to sing in tune while they navigate the voice change—no need to mention that breathy sound you're getting from the girls, it will get better). The entire chapter entitled "Tips for Nurturing the Singing Voice in Transition" published in 2010 by MENC (now NAfME) gives specific examples of how to help boys without a single mention of the female voice change.[17] Why would a middle school girl want to be fully engaged in a classroom whose teacher seems more concerned about boys than girls?

Thanks to the research completed by Lynne Gackle and others, we now have resources that specifically discuss the needs of the female changing voice. Even with this research, and even though the female voice change is now accepted as a biological fact, teachers—and pedagogical resources—continue to focus on the needs of the boys.[18] Separating choirs into single-sex classes allows teachers to directly guide singers through the voice change, providing specific and helpful feedback as well as educational parity.

Although Title IX legislation generally prohibits single-sex classes or activities in public schools, there is an allowance for single-sex choirs: "The current regulations permit [schools] . . . to make requirements based on vocal range or quality which may result in a chorus or choruses of one or predominantly one sex."[19]

Community-based choirs and private or parochial school choirs do not face the same legal constraints, as they do not receive federal funding (this discussion does not include the issues of educational vouchers used to attend private or parochial schools). Scheduling single-sex choir classes in public schools may prove a challenge for administrators, particularly in a smaller school where choir is not scheduled to meet daily, but Title IX also makes allowances for health classes where human sexuality is taught and for physical education classes where there may be bodily contact. These classes could be scheduled opposite choirs who do not meet every day. Many community children's choir programs separate girls and boys during the middle school years, then combine singers into SATB choirs after the voice change. Girl choir programs have the added benefit, however, of giving teachers the flexibility to address the voice change over a longer time frame. This is particularly important because girls are entering puberty at an increasingly young age.[20] A choir teacher in the United States is likely to hear a girl begin puberty between the ages of 8 and 14,[21] so separating choirs by sex is valuable even before the middle school years.

By way of example, the Lawrence Academy of Music Girl Choir program has multiple choirs overlapping the same age groups. Girls audition into each ensemble, but the audition does not just take musical skill level into account. Where singers are in the voice change may be the most important determining factor for their placement during grades four through eight. Five different ensembles (grades three-five, grades four-six, grades five-seven, grades six-eight, and grades eight-ten) address the different phases of the female voice change. The teacher of each ensemble selects repertoire appropriate for the girls' vocal stage, explains and demystifies the voice change process, and promotes a positive body image through repertoire selection and conversations about vocal and physical growth as the girls move through puberty. Depending upon the voice change, girls can remain in an ensemble for multiple years or move to another out of sequence. Each ensemble is viewed as both the scaffolding for older choirs as well as a destination in its own right. Each receives high quality instruction using repertoire that addresses the needs—both musical and social—of the girls in the ensemble. An additional, non-auditioned choir is available for girls in grades three-five, and a high school choir contains singers in grades ten-twelve who have settled into their young adult voice. Frequent collaborations with collegiate and adult ensembles help the high school singers remember that their voices, too, continue to grow and change as they mature into adulthood.

It is particularly helpful to have conversations about girls' growing bodies in single-sex groupings. As our voice is part of our body, it is difficult for a girl to separate the social pressure or judgment she feels about her growing body from the growth of her voice. These judgments directly impact a girl's confidence, as by middle school, body image becomes the single most important determinant of a girl's self-esteem.[22] If a teacher can use non-judgmental language, based in scientific fact, in regard to the female voice change, it helps a girl to understand that there should also be no judgment in regard to the other changes that are happening in her body. Frank conversations about the vocal change remove the taboo about talking about puberty.

Discussions about the voice change also provide an important entry point in a conversation about self-identification and labels. In her research on mindset, published in a book by the same name, Stanford professor Carol Dweck demonstrates that people with a growth mindset (the belief that they can get better at something by working hard) rather than a fixed mindset (the belief that capacities are born, and that certain talented people are the only ones who can succeed at certain skills) are more motivated to learn and succeed.[23] If a girl choir teacher integrates the language of growth mindset into rehearsals, rewarding effort more than talent, a girl will be rewarded for what she does rather than who or what she perceives herself to be. This can manifest in use of language during the rehearsal: "That chord isn't in tune . . . *yet*," "I really appreciate your effort in learning that tricky rhythm—let's try again," "You singers are so hard-working" (rather than "talented"). The use of words that demonstrate progress will encourage growth. (The Lawrence Academy Girl Choir's famous line is, "Do-overs are allowed and encouraged, in music and in life.") Allowing girls to see that they are not "stuck" in a role reminds them that labels are a matter of convenience, not truth. For instance, remind the girls that there are probably no true altos in the room, but that someone needs to sing the alto line. Then stop referring to that group of girls as "altos," but as "girls who sing the alto line."

In addition to the physical changes girls experience at this age, confidence levels shift. The AAUW study indicates that before age nine, girls and boys are about equal in their levels of confidence. From ages nine to fifteen, however, girls display an enormous loss of self-esteem, defined by AAUW as "how a person views her performance in areas where success is important to her and how she believes she is perceived by significant others (parents, teachers, peers)."[24] Fostering a growth mindset in a girl choir rehearsal helps a girl remember that her performance is not fixed, that she can change in ways she chooses, and that she will get better at a task with sustained effort. During the critical middle school years, this helps to create scaffolding that leads to success.

# IN CONCLUSION

Although Title IX was implemented more than 40 years ago, and although the AAUW study was published more than 20 years ago, girls continue to face challenges tied to their gender and sex. These challenges persist into adulthood, as evidenced by the Kay and Shipman study, among others. For instance, although girls have made significant strides in measures of science and math achievement since the AAUW study was published, they remain severely underrepresented in tech-intensive industries.[25] As arts educators, we can't change the culture within these industries, but we can tailor our repertoire, change our language, structure our choirs, and plan our lessons to specifically equip girls with the skills necessary to fight any institutional bias they may confront as adults.

This chapter was to present an argument supporting the need for girl choirs, but it also demonstrates that how we teach girl choirs is perhaps as important as, if not more than, why they should exist in the first place. Many girls who sing in children's choirs are gaining the confidence and competence needed to be successful, but a girl choir program that progresses from grade school through high school can specifically tailor its curricula to girls' needs. Girl choir programs can use mentoring and modeling between older and younger students, develop a curriculum related to the female voice change, and create a spiral curriculum that continually reinforces and supports girls' self-confidence.

If organized and taught well, girl choirs become places to experience support for and collaboration with girls, rather than competition between girls, at a crucial stage of life. It is powerful to create a safe space for girls to take risks, learn about their growing bodies, and sing music that celebrates all of the realities and possibilities in their current and future lives. It's a shame that the American Choral Directors Association, of which I am a proud member, still does not have a Girl Choir division for Repertoire and Standards. It does have Boychoir, Children's and Community Youth Choir, Women's Choir, and Male Choir divisions, but not one for girls. In this decision, we see the perpetuation of the view that a mixed ensemble is "good enough" for girls, but not for boys. We need girl choirs to help girls find their voice—their song, their identity, their power.

# BEHIND
# THE SCENES

## CHAPTER 12

# WHY COLLABORATIONS?

BY JUDITH HERRINGTON

Collaborations can be both an inspiration and a framework for artistic and educational growth. They can be described by the familiar equation "the whole is greater than the sum of its parts." However, successful collaborations go beyond that outcome, as the resulting product is not only greater than the sum of the individual participants, but the participants grow beyond their original contribution. With a carefully chosen and planned collaboration, I know that my singers will benefit and grow beyond the point at which they initially started.

My role as the director/conductor/educator of my organization and choral classroom is to define parameters, train for the skill level and flexibility needed, and carefully frame the experience for the greatest possible success. The result can be thrilling and inspiring, or it can be disappointing and frustrating. Consider the following to ensure a positive experience and outcome for all.

## DEFINING COLLABORATIONS

By its very nature, a choral ensemble is collaboration: people working together through a common purpose to create a product to be shared. Collaborations come in all sizes, shapes, purposes, and levels of effectiveness. They can become a key component of an organization's purpose, making a significant impact on the participants, the participating organizations, and the shared audience.

Frequently, collaboration is considered a merging of musical organizations in the performance of a major work, with full orchestra, in a beautiful concert hall with perfect acoustics. This is a thrilling opportunity, but only one of many collaboration possibilities. By exploring and extending the definition of collaboration, we will discover rich opportunities for growth, connection, and artistry.

The noun collaboration is defined as "teamwork," with synonyms listed as partnership, group effort, association, and alliance. Let's look at a broader definition to discover exciting opportunities for growth and deeper learning. In the early years of our organization, a chance meeting at an office supply store with Kathryn Habedank, co-founder of Northwest Sinfonietta, led to a conversation that set a significant course for our program. "Collaborations are a key component to successful arts organizations. There is a crossing of audiences as well as educational mergers that are valuable to the organizations as well as the community." This shared insight from a successful arts manager was significant to us and set the course for a tradition and core value that is the hallmark of our program today. As we have explored and sought these experiences, we have discovered the depth and richness of collaborative experiences.

## THE CHORAL CLASSROOM = THE CHORAL TEAM

Taking the definition of "teamwork" apart, we recognize that the choral rehearsal and the choral performance are both multi-layered collaborations. It is important to be intentional in recognizing and planning these components. In the traditional rehearsal format, the director sets the course, runs the rehearsal, directs the concert, and oversees the program. It is critical that the team (ensemble) works together, with rhythmic integrity, unified tone production concepts, shared artistic interpretation, etc.

By intentionally including the singer in the learning process, the rehearsal is efficient and the student is connected and more fully involved in the experience. We know that deeper learning occurs when singers are motivated, invested, and understand relevance. As choral educators, we must constantly seek techniques that give the individual singer an opportunity to participate with more engagement. Many teachers and conductors find that carefully worded questions can lead to a more invested student.

## Making It Work

Questions for awareness can be broad, specific to an individual or group, shared between section partners, or included in a written reflection:

- Where do you want to improve?

- What do we need to fix?

- How did you fix that?

- What did you notice in _____?

- Why would a composer _____?

- What is the challenge in this section?

- What did you do that worked?

- What do you notice in another section?

# BEYOND YOUR CHORAL CLASSROOM

Consider collaborations that combine choirs within your organization, school, and/or school district. Combining different age groupings can be an especially motivating experience.

## Making It Work

Planning is everything. Find music that is accessible to all groups, simplifying parts if needed. Often, these collaborations have limited rehearsal time. Careful preparation from each organization is vital. A visit from the performance conductor will unify your teaching and be a motivation for your singers. Confer with all conductors in advance to ensure that even the youngest singers can successfully accomplish the literature.

# GUEST SOLOISTS

Your choral color palette is increased by employing a guest soloist (instrumental or vocal). This is valuable for your programming, as your audience will enjoy the added instrumental color and your singers will listen more critically as they perform.

### Making It Work

Determine if you will be using a professional or student soloist. Use your preparation time to plan tempi, phrasing, and other interpretive decisions. Send the performer a contract that outlines the rehearsal time, concert time, performance dress, and fee. Include a copy of their part with tempi and dynamic markings. It is also helpful to send a copy of the choral octavo.

At the first rehearsal with the soloist, remember that the choir will be inclined to listen to the soloist with less focus on their music. It is useful to have the soloist play their part first, without the choir. Ask your singers if they can hear where their part fits in. In performance, be careful of placement of the soloist. Can they see the conductor? Do they need eye contact with the accompanist? How is the balance? How is the sound of the choral ensemble?

# GUEST CONDUCTOR/CLINICIAN

This learning opportunity is filled with possibilities. Your singers will learn new approaches, be inspired by another professional, and often hear the same message that they have heard from their own director coming from a different voice.

The professional growth opportunity for the artistic conducting staff is also immeasurable. Watching and listening to another conductor teach and conduct your singers will allow you to listen, watch, and appreciate your singers from a different view. Consider asking your guest conductor/clinician to give you conducting feedback. You will find your skills expanding and habits carefully reviewed. Perhaps most importantly, your singers will see you seeking growth with a desire to learn. What a valuable model you will be giving your singers!

## Making It Work

Send a copy of your literature so the guest conductor can anticipate your expectations. Share your goals, concerns and desires for your group. Be mindful of the passage of time during rehearsal. This is time for your students to work with an expert, and it's easy to lose time with long announcements or your own rehearsing, unless that is one of the pre-determined goals. Following the session, schedule one-on-one time for debriefing and added insight.

# GUEST COMPOSERS

What a thrill for a young musician to meet and learn from a composer. What a gift to a composer to hear their music performed and interact with the singers. For the composer, he or she will always learn from hearing their music rehearsed and performed. For singers, the opportunity to discuss the composition, the text, and purpose of the music is inspiring.

## Making It Work

In planning your rehearsal with a guest composer, be sure to allocate enough time for the composer to share background information about their composing work and the meaning of the text. Our young people are creative students in many areas (visual arts, performing arts, athletics, theater, writing, etc.), and they will find these discussions inspiring.

# COLLABORATION WITH OTHER YOUTH CHOIRS AND FESTIVALS

The time spent in planning and preparing for joint experiences with other choirs is valuable, since young people are often inspired to share music making with their peers. It is recommended that in planning these events, you give careful thought to the many components that are involved for its success:

- Are the collaborating organizations like-minded in their purposes? Are they similar in their tonal production? Are the singers' ages similar? Are the singers similar in their skill level?

- Consider if the literature can be used in your own programming. The investment of purchasing and rehearsing will be of more value if you can use it in your own program.

- Mix your singers up so they become acquainted, giving them time to visit with each other. It can be useful to make sure that singers are grouped with a buddy from their own choir for their own confidence. Be mindful of where you place boys, so that they have other boys with whom to share the experience. Plan your placements (being mindful of height) ahead of time so that valuable rehearsal time isn't lost with directors sorting this out at the last minute. It is helpful if the hosting choir director is in charge of the combined choir placement.

- If you are sharing the podium with another choir, be sure that each conductor has equal representation in front of the choir. (Your singers will notice!)

# ADULT PROFESSIONAL AND COMMUNITY ORGANIZATIONS

These collaborations will be inspiring for the adult musicians as well as your young singers. One of my favorite memories is watching my high school singers move into placement with the adult choir and watching them being welcomed by the adults. Our singers sang differently after that experience. They came back to their regular rehearsals with an adult model in their minds, having had an experience where their own musicianship was embraced and valued. What a great joy for an adult musician, to have the opportunity to encourage and support a young singer in this way! See notes above for preparation of collaboration.

Singing with an orchestra is particularly thrilling and challenging! Joint rehearsals are usually limited, so preparation on the choir's part will ensure flexibility and success.

## Making It Work

- Literature needs to be carefully chosen for the success of the musicians, as well as the concert programming.

- When preparing your choir, include careful attention to tempi and rhythmic integrity. Unknowingly, your piano accompanist will adjust to your individual style, but a large orchestra will need a more consistent approach to the performance.

- If you do not conduct your choral rehearsals with a baton, plan to use one for several rehearsals in preparation. Additionally, estimate the distance from the conductor's podium to the choir. If the choir is behind the orchestra, it can be an adjustment for your singer to watch and stay emotionally connected.

- Your singers must be secure in their entrances and releases.

- As the director, you are the advocate for your singers and responsible for making the experience effective for your singers. Most challenging is the matter of balance. In planning with the orchestra conductor, express concern for volume balance. Possible solutions are amplifying the choir with microphones, reducing the number of players, and requesting that the orchestra play a dynamic level lower than marked.

- Brief your singers to "mind their manners." Visiting conductors will teach your singers as if they are professionals, and your singers will need to respect the conductor with the same professionalism.

- During the rehearsal, have your score available. If your choir has their music memorized and the conductor gives directions based on score markings, singers will be confused. Be prepared to give a word cue or verse number to help them.

Collaborations come in many sizes, shapes, and combinations. Be clear in your purposes and intentions with each project. Be sure that these purposes are clear to the organization, and that they are based on a foundation of respect. Your goal as an artistic director, conductor, music leader, or teacher is to maximize the value for your singers and your organization. The result will be of great value and inspire you, your singers, your organization, and your audiences.

## CHAPTER 13

# RECRUIT, RETAIN, RESULTS, REWARDS

BY ROBYN LANA

## RECRUITING NEW SINGERS

Recruiting new singers into a choral program is a fluid challenge. As demands on families' time and opportunities for youth grow, people must become more selective about what they choose to participate in. This is true of community choirs and church choirs but, to some extent, also true of school choirs. The choral program must stay relevant while keeping high artistic and educational standards. When youth and parents experience a program that is not simply entertaining but challenging, rewarding, confidence building, educational, diverse, and character building, they will make it a priority in their lives. The investment of time and commitment must be earned and not assumed.

Marketing is defined as the action of promoting and selling goods or services. Traditional marketing has some value in the form of mailings, radio, and print media. Yet it has been found that, for programs serving youth, the most effective marketing is word of mouth: a recommendation from a teacher, a referral from another parent, or a student sharing their excitement and pride with friends. Gain endorsements from local educators, respected musicians, and news media. If there is a public radio station, it is possible they would do a short feature on the choir. Local news shows enjoy highlighting good things going on in the community and may offer their support through a brief feature story.

Finding ways for a choral program to be connected to the community so that others see and hear the ensemble—making them visible and active participants in the community—provides opportunities for parents and singers to share their excitement and the positive aspects of participation. Sing at a sporting event. Celebrate and support a groundbreaking for a new facility. Participate in Veterans Day activities. Sing at events in the city or town where the general public can learn of the program and the parents and singers can chat with others about their pride in the program.

Collaborating with other organizations provides new audiences for any program. In a school, this can be an arts fair or a joint performance with a local adult choir. For community choral programs, seek to collaborate with those that may not be an obvious fit. For example, reach out to a nearby college and offer to work together on a performance project. Investigate interest from art museums, dance companies, contemporary music ensembles, folk music groups, and other types of arts where the collaboration may be unconventional but of great benefit to all participants. Orchestras and other adult choirs are often eager to join forces with children's and youth choirs. Not only does this kind of performance offer a unique experience to the children as they explore a new color and energy on stage with adults, but it also brings new audience members to both organizations.

In many cities there are art consortiums, music consortiums, or even choral consortiums. Seek out members and, as a director, become a part of those associations. In Cincinnati, the Greater Cincinnati Choral Consortium collaborates in concert to support a non-profit that provides school supplies. In Seattle, the choral consortium collaborates on three consecutive days of concerts. These events offer marketing value beyond the cost of membership.

# RETENTION, RESULTS, AND REWARDS

Retaining singers is largely dependent on the teaching style and artistic ability of the conductor. Always be prepared for rehearsals. Know the scores and each voice part. Have a clear interpretation in mind; yet, always be flexible enough to shift with the artistry that grows with the ensemble. Enable the singers to be a part of the music-making process, not simply the instrument that is played by the musician waving their arms. Engage them throughout the process. Offer an environment where they can grow and take ownership.

In addition to social and collaborative opportunities that build allegiance and friendships in the choral program, setting up a mentoring system will allow a different aspect of ownership and leadership among choir members. Whether working in a multi-age program or a school, identifying singers who are strong role models—not only regarding musicianship but, most significantly, in maturity and leadership—will build ownership in the ensemble and a sense of pride in which the participants are invested in the final product.

Student leaders must adhere to a safe, welcoming environment in the choral classroom. Take care not to create a hierarchy in which the leaders are perceived to be valued above others, but set a standard of acceptance and mutual growth so that all may excel together. In a multi-age program, younger singers will strive to be like the identified leaders. In a school program, youth will want to replicate the positive attitude of the leaders. Mentors must sincerely demonstrate how to be inclusive while demonstrating rehearsal etiquette and focused enthusiasm.

When children and their parents experience positive, energized teaching in the choral classroom, they are willing to invest their time and financial commitment. When they see joy in the faces of other choir members, feel the pride and confidence that comes with participating in a fine children's choir program, and experience a safe and welcoming environment to learn in, the singers and their parents will be committed to the program and become voices in the community. Such rewards, for both singers and choral programs, are priceless.

## CHAPTER 14

# PREPARING THE CHOIR FOR LARGE WORKS AND GUEST CONDUCTORS

BY ROBYN LANA

Communication is the greatest factor of success when working with children and youth. Clear instructions, conducting gestures, and eye contact from the podium are all elements of communication in performance. Expectations, how to enter and exit the stage, how to sit and stand, what direction to face, how to stand in a relaxed manner so that blood may circulate, and arriving hydrated and nourished are all part of the teaching process when working with youth. The environment changes dramatically when working with guest conductors and other large ensembles, especially professional orchestras. In particular, young choristers rely on their leader for comfort and trust them during stressful times; however, when working on large works, one cannot always provide that comfort and security. When preparing for large works and collaborations, it is imperative that the choristers are mentally, musically, and physically prepared for success.

To facilitate this, the conductor must be as familiar with a score as they would if they were going to conduct themselves. Know biographical information about the composer as well as the history and significance of the work to be performed, and then share that with the choir. Educating them will both increase their connection to the music and nurture their desire to connect with similar works throughout their lives. If not provided, request score markings from the conductor. Those should include phrasing, cut-offs, dynamics, and all aspects of the performance that can be prepared in advance.

If collaborating with a large orchestra chorus as well, discuss the pronunciation of the text, so that the children and adults are unified in their presentation. Pronunciation could be dialect-based, based on the space, or a variation of the language, such as singing in Ecclesiastical Latin or German Latin. An artistic performance is partially reliant on the choir understanding the translation of the text. Often, a children's choir plays a specific role in a large work or is used for a specific color in the palette of sound. For example, in Mahler's Third Symphony, the children's voices should ring through the texture of sound as they proclaim the sound of the bells, partnering with a women's chorus and alto solo. Yet, in Berlioz's *Te Deum*, the children's chorus is referred to as a large, third choir, singing in unison and representing the people who add to the ritual of sacred music.

The children's chorus must be ready to respond to a new conductor. In preparation, experiment with the gesture, allowing the choir to experience singing with both a large, flamboyant model and a minute gesture. Encourage them to sing musically without direct eye contact from the conductor, adjusting to sudden and unexpected dynamic and tempo changes. If they are not accustomed to seeing a baton, be sure to bring that into rehearsal. Many orchestral conductors are ahead of the orchestra, purposely so. When the children are trained to respond instantly to the gesture, this is a very difficult adjustment for them, which could be magnified if they are not placed on the stage. Often, a children's choir will sing from a balcony for specific effect, or because the stage, complete with orchestra and adult chorus, does not allow space for the children to enter and exit easily.

In May 2013, the Cincinnati Children's Choir performed Britten's *War Requiem* with the Cincinnati Symphony Orchestra and the May Festival Chorus. The artistic vision of conductor James Conlon put the 85-voice youth choir in the second balcony, in the back of the house, snuggly fit into a large, arched doorway. The placement enabled the young voices to drift across Music Hall, adding a glorious color to the production. The vast distance from the stage made it impossible to follow the sound from the stage. There was a monitor to see the conductor, yet technology does not always provide a simultaneous view. The assistant director of the orchestra was also in the balcony on one side of the children's choir conductor, while the portative organ was on the other side. The choir was in front of the children's choir conductor and the stage was directly behind. Quite literally, those contributing to the sound surrounded the children's choir conductor on all sides. The children needed to be prepared for any setting, mentally, visually, and physically in order for the performance to be a success.

It is helpful for the children to hear the work in advance. Ask the orchestra team if there is a previous recording of the work or if there is a recording that the maestro feels is an excellent example. Help the children hear what instrument plays their entrances. Being familiar with the new timbre when they are used to getting pitches from the piano, whether directly or from the orchestral reduction, will help the choristers be successful from the start. Likewise, knowing what instrument doubles their part and when to listen for it will be a valuable tool for the children. As much as possible, break down what the children will hear into elemental pieces, thus enabling them to be active participants in the rehearsals from the start, not simply youth trying to "catch up" to the professionals.

If the score is something that can be memorized, it is strongly recommended to do so. Holding bulky folders, especially while standing and sitting, can be cumbersome for small bodies. If it is not possible to memorize, practice how to hold the folders while also watching the conductor. The Cincinnati Children's Choir had 130 youth in the balcony of Cincinnati Music Hall performing Mahler's Eighth Symphony. The work is very difficult to memorize, so the children used scores. But in preparation, they had to be nearly memorized and, in some sections fully memorized, so that they could easily watch the maestro. The distance from the orchestra and the stage provided a challenge complicated by holding the scores. Compounding that, they needed to angle their bodies and point their voices out across the house, not simply to the stage, making eye contact with the maestro that much more difficult. Because they were so well prepared, ready to be flexible, and memorized in the most challenging section, they were able to adjust and present a successful performance.

Orchestral conductors will treat the children as professionals. When possible, collect the standing and sitting cues in advance and have the children write them in their scores. Practice how to stand and sit. Children and youth rarely perform with seats. They must be still, attentive, and sit with their knees together—no crossed legs. Scores should stay flat in their lap and open to the correct page. All pages should be marked, particularly if using a thick choral score. And most importantly, children should remain silent in rehearsal.

Particularly when working with a union orchestra, every minute is money. There is no tolerance for chatting. It is possible that the orchestral conductor will not have a strong comfort level working with youth. When the children respond professionally, they will ease the concerns of the maestro. During the full rehearsals, the children's choir conductor must be present and attentive with score in hand, to address issues and communicate with the conductor when necessary. Advocate for your choir, giving the maestro feedback on balance and other musical challenges or successes as the rehearsal moves forward.

Collaborating on large works is an experience that few youth have the opportunity to experience. It can be exciting to work with professional musicians, soloists, and prominent artists. In 2014, the Cincinnati Children's Choir shared the stage with John Morris Russell and the Cincinnati Pops. The children were on narrow risers, ten rows high, at the front edge of the stage. The top row was nearly even with the first balcony. They were required to stand in this human tower formation for a full hour. Yet, they never uttered a word of complaint. The children quickly realized that they had the best seats in the house! Not only could they see the full concert, they could enjoy the facial expressions of John Morris Russell as he worked. They had an almost bird's-eye view of the instrumentalists. When guest artists and dancers, including a Broadway star, entered the stage, not only did they sing with them, they could nearly reach out and touch them, such was their proximity.

Preparing for large collaborations often gives young singers exposure to music and experiences that we cannot produce on our own in our small programs. It is worth the effort and preparation to help them be successful and proud of their performance. They will earn the respect of the arts community and future collaborations will be available to the next generation of choristers.

# APPENDICES

# NOTES

## Chapter One

1. Sharp, Timothy W. *Mentoring in the Ensemble Arts: Helping Others Find Their Voice.*
   Chicago: GIA Publications, Inc., 2014.

## Chapter Three

1. Gardner, Howard. *Frames of Mind: The Theory of Multiple Intelligences.* New York: Basic
   Books, 1983.

## Chapter Four

1. Frazee, Jane. *Discovering Keetman.* Mainz: Schott Music, 1998.

2. Wang, Cecilia Chu, and D. Gregory Springer. *Orff Schulwerk: Reflections and Directions.*
   Chicago: GIA Publications, Inc., 2013.

3. Gray, Cynthia. "The Wise Old Owl." Santa Barbara Music Publishing #1159.

4. Mann, Rochelle, and C. Scott Hagler. "I'm Gonna Sing When the Spirit Says Sing." Colla Voce
   Music, Inc. #35-96360. © 2011 Colla Voce Music, Inc. International Copyright Secured. All
   Rights Reserved. Used with Permission.

## Chapter Five

1. Cleveland, Susan. "Developing Inner Hearing through the Twelve Skills Areas." *Kodály
   Envoy* 33, 3 (2007): 25.

2. Gordon, Edwin. "Tonal Syllables: A Comparison of Purposes and Systems." In D. Walters and C. Taggert (Eds.), *Readings in Music Learning Theory*. Chicago: GIA Publications, 1989. 66–71.

3. Kodály, Zoltan. Introduction to the volume "Musical Education in Hungary". In F. Bónis (Ed.), *The Selected Writing of Zoltan Kodály*. London: Boosey & Hawkes, 1974. 206.

4. Eisen, Ann, and Lamar Robertson. *An American Methodology*. Lake Charles: Sneaky Snake Publications, 2002.

5. Nemes, Klara. "The Relative Sol-Fa as a Tool of Developing Musical Thinking." *Zoltan Kodály: Composer, Musicologist, and Educationist–A Festschrift for Professor Matti Vainio*. Finland: Jyväskylän Yliopisto, 1996.

6. Palkki, Joshua. "Rhythm Syllable Pedagogy: A Historical Journey to Takadimi via the Kodály Method." *Journal of Music Theory Pedagogy* 24 (2010): 101–129.

7. Krueger, Carol J. *Progressive Sight Singing*. New York: Oxford University Press, 2007.

8. Kodály, Zoltan. "Let Us Sing Correctly." Boosey & Hawkes #M060035388/48009982. © 1952 Boosey & Hawkes, Ltd. All Rights Reserved. Reprinted with Permission.

9. Stroope, Z. Randall. "Inscription of Hope." Heritage Music Press #15/1081H-3. © 1993 Heritage Music Press, a division of The Lorenz Corporation. All Rights Reserved. International Copyright Secured. Reprinted with Permission.

10. Friedersdorf, Jill, and Melissa Malvar-Keylock. "Quiet Sea." Colla Voce Music, Inc. #24-96545. © 2009 Colla Voce Music, Inc. International Copyright Secured. All Rights Reserved. Used with Permission.

11. Britten, Benjamin. *Missa Brevis in D*. Boosey & Hawkes #060014703/48008948. © 1959 Boosey & Hawkes, Ltd. All Rights Reserved. Reprinted with Permission

ADDITIONAL READING:

Demorest, Steven. *Building Choral Excellence: Teaching Sight-Singing in the Choral Rehearsal*. New York: Oxford University Press, 2001.

Demorest, Steven. "Integrating Sight-Singing into the High School Choral Rehearsal." *Choral Journal* 39, 5 (1998): 55–58.

# Chapter Seven

1. Sharp, Timothy W. *Collaboration in the Ensemble Arts: Working and Playing Well with Others*. Chicago: GIA Publications, Inc., 2014.

# Chapter Eight

1. Kesselman, Lee. "The Friendly Beasts." Colla Voce Music, Inc. #20-96510.

# Chapter Nine

1. Phillips, Kenneth H. *Directing the Choral Music Program*. New York: Oxford University Press, 2004.

## Chapter Ten

1. Leck, Henry. "The Boys ~~Changing~~ Expanding Voice: Take The High Road." *Choral Journal* 49, 11 (2009): 49–60.

2. Leck, Henry. *The Boy's Changing Voice: Take The High Road.* Milwaukee: Hal Leonard Corporation, 2001. Video.

3. Freer, Patrick K. "Foundation of the Boy's Expanding Voice: A Response to Henry Leck." *Choral Journal* 50, 7 (2010): 29–35.

ADDITIONAL READING:

Ackerley, Julian. "Motivate with Mottos." *Choral Journal* 49, 9 (2008): 78–79.

Ackerley, Julian. "The Boy Singer." *Choral Journal* 50, 4 (2009): 64–65.

Asley, Martin. *How High Should Boys Sing? Gender, Authenticity, and Credibility in the Young Male Voice.* Farnham: Ashgate Publishing, 2009.

Autry, James. *The Servant Leader.* Roseville: Prima Publishing, 2001.

Barham, Terry J. *Strategies for Teaching Junior High and Middle School Male Singers.* Santa Barbara: Santa Barbara Music Publishing, 2001.

Barham, Terry J. and Darolyne L. Nelson. *The Boy's Changing Voice: New Solutions for Today's Choral Teacher.* Miami: Belwin, Inc., 1991.

Gurian, Michael. *The Wonder of Boys.* New York: Penguin Group, 1996.

Harrison, Scott D. "Engaging Boys–Overcoming Stereotypes." *Choral Journal* 45, 2 (2004): 25–29.

Kindlon, Dan and Michael Thompson. *Raising Cain: Protecting the Emotional Life of Boys.* New York: Ballantine Books, 2000.

Meeker, Meg. *Boys Should Be Boys.* New York: Ballantine Books, 2008.

Metzl, Jordan M.D. and Carol Shookhoff, Ph.D. *The Young Athlete: A Sports Doctor's Complete Guide for Parents.* New York: Little, Brown and Company Publisher, 2003.

Sheehy, Harry and Danny Peary. *Raising a Team Player: Teaching Kids Lasting Values on the Field, on the Court, and on the Bench.* North Adams: Story Books Publishing, 2002.

Swanson, Frederick J. *Music Teaching in the Junior High and Middle School.* Englewood Cliffs: Prentice-Hall, Inc., 1973.

Journal Buddies. "Improve Your Boy's Self Esteem in Just Minutes a Day." http://www.journalbuddies.com/index_boys.htm [2009].

## Chapter Eleven

1. American Association of University Women Educational Foundation. *How Schools Shortchange Girls*, executive summary. 1992, 2.

2. Ibid., 3.

3. Ibid., 7.

4. Orenstein, Peggy. *Schoolgirls: Young Women, Self-Esteem, and the Confidence Gap*. New York: Anchor Books, 2000, xvi.

5. Kay, Katty and Claire Shipman. "Closing the Confidence Gap." *The Atlantic*. May (2014): 64.

6. Runfola, Marie, ed. and Joanne Rutkowski, ed. *Tips: The Child Voice*. Lanham, MD: Rowman & Littlefield Education, 2010, 43.

7. Orenstein, Peggy. *Schoolgirls: Young Women, Self-Esteem, and the Confidence Gap*. New York: Anchor Books, 1994, 36.

8. Ibid., 68.

9. Kay and Shipman, "Closing the Confidence Gap," 59.

10. President's Committee on the Arts and the Humanities. *Reinvesting in Arts Education: Winning America's Future Through Creative Schools*, 2011, 16.

11. Kay and Shipman, "Closing the Confidence Gap," 64.

12. President's Committee on the Arts and the Humanities, 18.

13. Ibid.

14. Kay and Shipman, "Closing the Confidence Gap," 66.

15. American Association of University Women Educational Foundation, 7.

16. Lamb, Sharon. *The Secret Lives of Girls: What Good Girls Really Do–Sex Play, Aggression, and Their Guilt*. New York: The Free Press, 2001, 203.

17. Runfola and Rutkowski, ed., 43–48.

18. O'Toole, Patricia. "A Missing Chapter from Choral Methods Books: How Choirs Neglect Girls." *Choral Journal* 39, 5 (1998): 29.

19. U.S. Department of Education. *Guidelines Regarding Single Sex Classes and Schools*. http://www2.ed.gov/about/offices/list/ocr/t9-guidelines-ss.html [October 29, 2014].

20. Gackle, Lynne. *Finding Ophelia's Voice, Opening Ophelia's Heart: Nurturing the Adolescent Female Voice*. Dayton, OH: Heritage Music Press, 2011, 15.

21. Ibid.

22. Orenstein, Peggy. *Cinderella Ate My Daughter*. New York: Harper Collins, 2011, 137–138.

23. Dweck, Carol S. *Mindset: The New Psychology of Success*. New York: Ballantine Books, 2006.

24. American Association of University Women Education Foundation, xx–xxiii.

25. Beninger, Anna. "High Potentials in Tech-Intensive Industries: The Gender Divide in Business Roles." *Catalyst Research Centers Report* (2014).

# SAMPLE FORMS

# CINCINNATI CHILDREN'S CHOIR CORE VALUES

### Education

The Cincinnati Children's Choir provides a learning environment that is creative and nurturing. Singers are informed and reflective, building upon their knowledge and musical understanding, as they become independent musicians.

### Community

The Cincinnati Children's Choir provides entertaining programming of artistic and cultural merit that promotes unity and understanding between people of varied backgrounds. CCC strives to support the greater Cincinnati community by providing training and networking opportunities for music professionals, providing choral opportunities for children in far reaching suburbs, and collaborating with various cultural organizations.

### Inclusiveness

The Cincinnati Children's Choir provides a safe haven for young singers. Through the welcoming environment, each child is valued and accepted. Need-based tuition assistance is made available throughout the year and outreach programs are developed to meet children in their communities focusing on underserved. Singers explore diversity in repertoire performed and membership, building personal friendships with others outside of their community.

### Excellence

Through passionate and inspiring education and consistent evaluation, the Cincinnati Children's Choir demonstrates artistry that is dynamic and respectful of historical and world music.

### Collaboration

The Cincinnati Children's Choir enjoys collaborating with area music educators, composers, and arts organizations. Joint ventures enable a greater exposure of CCC to the community and provide our singers with invaluable learning opportunities.

### Innovation

The Cincinnati Children's Choir continually seeks to provide relevant and exciting programming to the greater Cincinnati area, as well as to the national and international choral community. Through regional, national, and international festivals, commissions, composition competitions, and opportunities for area educators, CCC strives to be at the forefront of choral music.

### Confidence

Participation in the program fosters joyful fulfillment, a sense of achievement, increased independence, confidence, and leadership qualities in our choristers.

### Integrity

The Cincinnati Children's Choir operates with responsibility and accountability to those who support and collaborate with the program whether they are stakeholders, volunteers, donors, or families. We honor these relationships and realize the importance of open and honest communication.

# CHOIR PARENT CODE OF CONDUCT

The board and staff have implemented the following Choir Parent Code of Conduct. The Code demonstrates important messages about the proper role of parents in supporting their child in the arts. Parents should read, understand, and sign this form prior to their child's participation. Any parent who breaks this Code of Conduct at any concert or rehearsal will be asked to leave the facility. Repeat violations may cause an extended period of suspension.

## Six Pillars of Character

The essential elements of character building and ethics in choral art are embodied in the concept of acceptable conduct and six core principles:

- Trustworthiness
- Respect
- Responsibility
- Fairness
- Caring
- Good citizenship

Member singers will reach their highest potential when participation reflects these six "pillars of character." I therefore agree:

1. I will support my child's choice to participate in choir.

2. I will remember that children participate to have fun and learn through positive experiences. Through this, high artistry can be achieved.

3. I will demonstrate respect for the director, staff, and volunteers.

4. I (and my guests) will be a positive role model for my child. I will be encouraging by showing respect and courtesy and by demonstrating positive support for all singers, directors, staff, volunteers, and audience members.

5. I (and my guests) will not engage in any kind of negative conduct with any singer, director, singer, volunteer, or parent.

6. I will not encourage any behaviors or practices that would belittle the singers, directors, staff, or volunteers.

7. I will demand that my child treat other singers, directors, staff, and volunteers with respect regardless of race, creed, color, sex, or ability.

8. I will teach my child that doing one's best is most important, so that my child will never feel undervalued.

9. I will emphasize and support the benefit of musicianship skill development and the learning and team building that goes on in rehearsals.

10. I will respect the directors and their authority during rehearsals and concerts. I will never question, discuss, or confront directors in front of other singers and families, and will take time to speak with directors privately at an arranged agreed upon time and place.

11. I will address concerns with the director of the choir directly before bringing concerns to others. If I do not receive a response, I will address my concerns with the artistic director. If I do not receive a response, I will address my concerns to the parent liaison serving on the board of directors.

12. I understand that my responsibilities include setting an example for children and that any breech of those responsibilities will result in my inability to attend rehearsals or performances, if deemed necessary by the administrative or artistic staff or the board of directors.

_____               _____
Parent/Guardian Signature                                               Date

# SINGER CODE OF CONDUCT

The following policies will be enforced for the children's safety and in order to achieve productive, professional quality rehearsals out of respect for each other. Failure to comply with these policies could result in dismissal from the choir.

## Rehearsal Guidelines and Dress Code

1. *The choir maintains a respectful environment and is a safe place for all singers. Any singer or parent in violation of this policy will be considered for immediate dismissal.*

2. Arrive no more than ten minutes before the scheduled rehearsal time and immediately check-in with your choir manager or student intern. Late arrivals must always check-in before taking their seat. If tardy, please be sure the singer has a note from a parent.

3. Give any attendance notes, permission slips, etc. to the choir manager at the check-in table.

4. Do not hand any payments to your conductor or artistic staff.

5. Do not roam the building or campus at any time. Stay in the rehearsal area.

6. Do not bring food or drinks into the rehearsal area. A tightly sealed water bottle containing water will be permitted.

7. At all times, show respect for each other, parent volunteers, and the facilities.

8. Pay attention to the director at all times and do not talk or in any way distract other singers.

9. We are guests of CCM and any other venue in which we rehearse or perform. Please do not run, yell, or demonstrate any other disrespectful behavior.

10. Always bring your choir bag, music, pencil, and handouts given by the director.

11. Do not fold or roll music.

12. All markings should be made lightly.

13. Folders and music are the singers' responsibility. If folders and music are lost or irreparably damaged, there will be a $25 replacement charge.

14. Choir members will be regularly responsible for carrying their music and studying outside of rehearsal, if necessary. Occasionally, scores will not be allowed to leave the rehearsal room. This is to ensure that the music is not lost and most often occurs with orchestral and rented scores. Parents are always welcome to come to rehearsal or read through a score.

15. Singers are responsible for delivering handouts, calendars, and other written information to their parents promptly!

16. If a singer is unable to actively participate in the rehearsal, he or she should still bring all necessary materials and observe quietly. It will benefit the singer to quietly listen when experiencing a minor illness, rather than stay home and miss rehearsal completely. Additionally, research has proven that those who sing through colds and minor illnesses encounter shorter, less-severe symptoms.

17. Shirts and tops must be long enough to tuck into pants and must have necklines high enough to cover cleavage and shoulders.

18. Clothing that has profanity, sexual innuendoes or overtones, promotes drugs, alcohol, or tobacco products, makes reference to gang-related, satanic, or cult-like activity, or promotes violence is not appropriate for choir activities.

# SINGER CODE OF CONDUCT
*(continued)*

## Performance Guidelines

1. Singers should always eat a nutritious meal and get plenty of rest before a performance.

2. Singers should use the restroom before arriving at the concert site.

3. Singers should arrive ten minutes before the scheduled call and check in with the choir manager or student intern.

4. If a singer is late for the scheduled call, the singer may be excluded from the concert.

5. All singers should arrive dressed for the performance as listed in the performance detail sheet provided on our website.

6. Singers should remain calm, quiet, and professional and give the director and/or performance coordinator their undivided attention.

7. All singers must demonstrate artistic understanding of the performance repertoire. Failure to demonstrate this at the final dress rehearsal may result in the singer being excluded from that concert.

8. All singers must demonstrate that the music has been fully memorized prior to the dress rehearsal, unless otherwise noted by the conductor.

9. If a singer feels ill during a performance, he or she should sit down where he or she is standing. If the singer is feeling better at the end of the song, he or she may stand up again. If not, he or she should quietly leave the stage. There will be parent volunteers watching and ready to assist. For his or her own safety, once a singer leaves the stage, the singer may not return to the stage.

10. *Please remember that the singers are representing the choir and, at times, our city and the United States of America. Best behavior is expected.*

# AUTHOR BIOGRAPHIES

## ROBYN LANA

Robyn Lana is the Founder, Managing Artistic Director, and Conductor of the Cincinnati Children's Choir (CCC), Ensemble-in-Residence at the University of Cincinnati College-Conservatory of Music Preparatory Department (CCM), serves on the choral faculty at Xavier University, and has served on the adjunct choral faculty at CCM. Under her leadership, CCC earned a gold medal in the 2012 World Choir Games, coming in first in the United States in their category. In December 2015, CCC received the prestigious American Prize for Choral Performance in Youth Choirs. In June 2016, CCC received the Chorus America ASCAP Award for Adventurous Programming.

A leading clinician and conductor across the US, Lana has been invited to present and conduct internationally. Invitations include China, Italy, Japan, and Malaysia. Lana has conducted international, state, and regional honor and festival choirs throughout the United States including Florida, Georgia, Kentucky, Indiana, Mississippi, New Jersey, New York, North Carolina, Ohio, Pennsylvania, South Carolina, Tennessee, Washington, Wisconsin, Wyoming, and the American Choral Directors Association (ACDA) Southern Division. She has been a featured guest conductor at Carnegie Hall, Beijing's Forbidden City Concert Hall, St. Peter's Basilica in Rome and will have her Kennedy Center debut in 2017. She has presented workshops for ACDA, the American Orff Schulwerk Association (AOSA)

National Conference, Chorus America, the World Choir Games 2012, National Association for Music Education (NAfME) state and regional conventions (Arizona, Indiana, Mississippi, New Jersey, New York, Ohio, Pennsylvania, Tennessee, Wisconsin, and Wyoming), the Chamber Music America National Convention, and regionally at colleges and universities. Her choirs have performed for state, regional, and national professional development conferences including the ACDA National Conference, the ACDA Central Division, and the AOSA National Conference.

Lana regularly prepares her choirs for collaborations with the Cincinnati Symphony, the Cincinnati Pops, the Cincinnati May Festival, and CCM choirs and orchestras achieving an extensive list of orchestral and operatic repertoire for children and praise from collaborating conductors including John Adams, Louis Langree, John Morris Russell, Marcus Huber, James Conlon, Earl Rivers, and Mark Gibson, among others. Lana has prepared CCC for two Telarc label recordings with the Cincinnati Pops Orchestra under the direction of Maestro Erich Kunzel.

Lana is the editor of a choral series in her name with Santa Barbara Music Publishing. The highly successful series has become respected throughout the national choral community. She has published articles in ACDA's *Choral Journal*, Choristers Guild's *The Chorister*, and Chamber Music America's *CMA Matters*.

Lana served as an ACDA representative for the 2012 World Choir Games Music Advisory Committee. From 2007–2013, she served ACDA as National Chair for Children's and Community Youth Choir Repertoire and Standards. In her work for ACDA, she pioneered the national committee into innovative project to serve membership. She established the now biennial conference for children's and community youth choir directors and initiated specific networking opportunities at the national conference. She currently serves ACDA as the Chair of the Standing Committee on Advocacy and Collaboration and is on the board of Chorus America.

A founding board member of the Greater Cincinnati Choral Consortium, she served as president of the board from 2013–2016. She earned both bachelor's and master's degrees in music education from the University of Cincinnati College-Conservatory of Music and holds Level III Orff Schulwerk Certification. With a focus in choral conducting, Lana earned a cognate in voice and has done post-graduate studies at Butler University. She is a recent recipient of CCM's Distinguished Alumna Award.

---

## JULIAN ACKERLEY

Dr. Julian Ackerley has achieved acclaim as an accomplished conductor and administrator of choral organizations. He has been Director of the Tucson Arizona Boys Chorus since 1980, taking the choristers on performance tours spanning five continents and over 25 countries. He is also Director of Music at St. Francis de Sales Church in Tucson.

Ackerley served as the National Boychoir Repertoire and Standards Chair for the American Choral Directors Association (ACDA) and is a specialist in working with boys' emerging voices. He was selected Choral Director of the Year by the ACDA Arizona Chapter. He is an experienced teacher, having taught music at all levels from elementary to university students.

Ackerley received his doctor of musical arts degree from the University of Arizona with emphasis in music education, vocal performance, and choral conducting. He is a frequent guest conductor and clinician at choral festivals and all-state choirs.

Through the years, his choirs have received numerous prestigious invitations to appear in regional, national and international conferences and festivals.

## KAREN BRUNO

Karen Bruno has been Director of the Academy since 2010 and a member of its teaching staff since 1996. In addition to her administrative duties, she teaches the Bel Canto Girl Choir singers and is the artistic director of the Girl Choir program. She received bachelor's degrees in both economics and music from Smith College, a teaching certificate from Lawrence University's Conservatory of Music, and a master's of music degree in music education from Boston University. She has taught choral music in the Appleton and Oshkosh school districts and at an international school in Senegal, West Africa. Bruno has been a guest speaker and adjunct professor in a variety of Lawrence Conservatory music education classes and has served as both cooperating and practicum teacher for students from Lawrence and St. Norbert College.

As a guest conductor, Bruno has been invited to work with the South Dakota All-State Children's Choir, numerous regional honor choirs, the Singing in Wisconsin festival, and is a past staff member of the Wisconsin School Music Association's Treble Honor Choir. She served for six years as the repertoire and standards chair for Children's and Community Youth Choirs in the North Central Division of the American Choral Directors Association (ACDA), is a member of the VoiceCare Network, and serves on the committee advocating the Comprehensive Musicianship through Performance (CMP) teaching model. She represents the Academy within the Fox Arts Network, writes an arts-focused column several times per year for the *Post Crescent* newspaper and has served on music scholarship selection committees on behalf of the Community Foundation for the Fox Valley Region.

Bruno is a two-time recipient of the WCDA's Five-Star Award, a recipient of Lawrence University's Pi Kappa Lambda award for excellence in music education, a Rotary Scholarship Award winner and was recognized by the Danbury (CT) Music Centre for providing outstanding musical opportunities for youth in the United States. Under her tutelage, Bel Canto was awarded Second Place in the national American Prize competition and has performed, by invitation, on state and divisional conventions of choral conductors.

## JAN CORROTHERS

Jan Corrothers is a collaborative pianist and organist based in the Greater Nashville region where she serves as a full-time staff accompanist for the music department of Austin Peay State University in Clarksville, Tennessee.

In demand as a collaborative pianist, Corrothers performs as accompanist for many choral conventions, workshops, festivals, and reading sessions across the United States and abroad, and collaborates regularly with the Festival Singers of Florida, under the direction of Dr. Kevin Fenton. She has presented workshops on the art of choral collaboration for organizations including Chorus America, the Fellowship of American Baptist Musicians, and in Beijing, China.

Previously, Corrothers held positions as staff accompanist and lecturer of music at Xavier University, Northern Kentucky University, Alderson Broaddus University and Marietta College. She also served as principal accompanist of the award-winning Cincinnati

Children's Choir, in residence at the University of Cincinnati College-Conservatory of Music, under the direction of Robyn Lana, from 2006–2016.

Jan received a master's of music degree in organ performance from the Shenandoah University Conservatory of Music and a bachelor's of arts degree in organ performance and church music from Alderson Broaddus University. In 2008, Jan was the recipient of the Alderson Broaddus University Outstanding Young Alumni Award.

## EVA FLOYD

Dr. Eva Floyd is an associate professor of choral music education at University of Cincinnati College-Conservatory of Music (CCM) where she teaches Choral Methods, Literature for School Choir, Voice Class, History and Philosophy of Music Education, and Kodály Musicianship. Dr. Floyd supervises student teachers, choral internships, advises graduate research, and is an academic advisor for undergraduate vocal/piano music education majors.

Dr. Floyd is a specialist in the Kodály approach of choral music education, which is based on the internationally acclaimed Hungarian system of teaching music literacy and ear-training. Dr. Floyd studied two years at the Liszt Academy's Kodály Pedagogical Institute of Music in Kecskemét, Hungary studying with Peter Erdei and earning an advanced diploma in choral conducting. Floyd also worked as a graduate teaching assistant at the Kodály Institute, tutoring international students in solfege and assisting graduate students with thesis projects. Currently, Floyd is the Midwestern Regional Representative to the Organization of American Kodály Educators National Board.

Floyd received a Ph.D. in music education and a master's of music in music education with choral conducting emphasis from University from Kentucky and a bachelor's of music in music education from Campbellsville University. Floyd completed Orff Schulwerk certification at the University of Kentucky and Kodály training at Capital University, where she also completed the Kodály apprentice teacher-training program.

Dr. Floyd's articles have been published in NAfME's (National Association for Music Education) publications such as *Update: Applications of Research in Music Education*, *The Journal of Music Teacher Education*, *The Choral Journal*, *Kodály Envoy*, *American Music Teacher*, and the *Bulletin of the Internal Kodály Society*. She has presented her research at Kentucky and Ohio Music Educators Association conferences, the American Choral Directors regional conference, Society for Music Teacher Education national conferences, and International Symposia in Scotland, Hungary, Poland, Australia, and Greece.

## JUDITH HERRINGTON

Judith Herrington is the Founder and Artistic Director of the highly acclaimed Tacoma Youth Chorus. She brings more than 40 years of teaching and conducting experience to her work at Charles Wright Academy in Tacoma, Washington, and is a recipient of the Inspirational Faculty Award and Murray Foundation Chair for Teaching Excellence.

Herrington is highly regarded as a guest conductor, workshop, and state and regional honor choir conductor, and served as visiting faculty at VanderCook College of Music. She is a past president and recipient of the leadership and service award of the Washington American Choral Directors Association and member of the Washington Music Educators Association Hall of Fame. Through Pavane Publishing, Colla Voce Publishing, and Hal Leonard, she has published choral compositions, arrangements, and choral teaching texts. She also edits several choral series for Pavane Publishing.

## JOSHUA PEDDE

As Artistic Director for the Indianapolis Children's Choir, Joshua Pedde is the principal director of the ICC's most advanced treble choirs and has been instrumental in growing the ICC's Innovations program, which provides free music education workshops to public and private schools.

Pedde is a frequent conductor throughout the United States, including the Kennedy Center and Lincoln Center. He has conducted at numerous sporting events and has traveled throughout Europe preparing and conducting choirs for performances at the Vatican, as well as in England, Italy, Austria, Spain, Germany, and Ireland.

He serves as chair for the Consortium of Indiana Children's Choirs, assistant director of worship and organist at Carmel Lutheran Church, and director of the Carmel Community Choir and Orchestra. He earned his bachelor's and master's degrees from Butler University, and a doctorate of pastoral music from Concordia University.

## SANDRA THORNTON

Sandra Thornton is the Assistant Artistic Director of the Cincinnati Children's Choir, Ensemble-In-Residence at the University of Cincinnati College-Conservatory of Music, where she conducts the Vivace, Allegro, and Cincinnati Girl Choirs within the program and serves as the Artistic Director of the Satellite Program. Additionally, she teaches Vocal Pedagogy during the annual CCC Summer Festival. She is also the Director of Traditional Music at Epiphany United Methodist Church in Loveland, Ohio, and is a professional singer with the Cincinnati Vocal Arts Ensemble, under the direction of Craig Hella Johnson.

A native of Syracuse, New York, Thornton received a bachelor's of music in music education from the Crane School of Music at the State University of New York at Potsdam and a master's of music in choral conducting from the Cincinnati College-Conservatory of Music. She has taught in Texas, Louisiana, and Ohio. Choirs under her direction have consistently received superior ratings at regional and state level choral competitions. In 2013, Thornton made her Carnegie Hall conducting debut with the Anderson High School Mixed Chorus. In demand as a clinician and guest conductor, Thornton has directed honor choirs in New York, Ohio, and Kentucky, and will be joining the faculty of the Fellowship of American Baptist Musicians (FABM) in the summer of 2017 to serve as the Children's Choir Clinician for the FABM Conference for Church Musicians.

She was the recipient of the Joy Anthony Douglas ('56) Master Teacher Residency at the Crane School of Music in 2012 and was awarded the SUNY Potsdam Alumni Association Rising Star Award in 2013. Additionally, in 2013, Thornton was a quarterfinalist for the first ever GRAMMY Foundation Music Educator of the Year Award.

Thornton currently serves as the Children's and Community Youth Choir Central Division Chair for the American Choral Director's Association and as Education Chair for the Greater Cincinnati Choral Consortium. Her professional affiliations include the American Choral Directors Association and the National Association for Music Education.

## ANTHONY TRECEK-KING

Anthony Trecek-King is the Artistic Director of the award-winning Boston Children's Chorus (BCC). Under his direction, the chorus has earned a reputation as an ensemble of high distinction and in 2013 received the National Arts and Humanities Youth Program award from the White House. Trecek-King's performances have been heralded as possessing a "surprising range of dynamics and depth of expression." He has collaborated on performances with Keith Lockhart, John Williams, Simon Halsey, Yo Yo Ma, Leslie Odom Jr., and Melinda Doolittle, and conducted many all-state and festival choirs in the United States and beyond.

Trecek-King also hosted the choral music radio program "Together in Song," presented two talks for TEDx Boston, and plays host on the choral music television series "Sing That Thing." He holds a bachelor's of music in cello performance from the University of Nebraska at Omaha, a master's of music in orchestral conducting from Florida State University, and a doctorate of musical arts in choral conducting from Boston University.